Fragments Of A Mirror
Selected Essays

Knud Sønderby

Translated from Danish by
Michael Goldman

Spuyten Duyvil
New York City

Sincere appreciation to The Danish Arts Foundation for their financial support towards the translation and publication of this book. Sincere appreciation as well to Gyldendal Publishing, Copenhagen, for their cooperation in the translation and publication of this book.

THE DANISH ARTS FOUNDATION

©Knud Sønderby & Gyldendal, Copenhagen. Published by agreement with Gyldendal Group Agency.
Translation ©2017 Michael Goldman
ISBN 978-1-944682-36-1

Library of Congress Cataloging In Publication Data applied for.

to Jette

Contents

ix	Preface
xi	Translator's Introduction
1	Addiction to speed
8	The Black Swan
18	Deer Park in the Dark
24	Encounter with the Dark
30	The Glint of Blue
37	The Hawthorns
42	A Ride with a Lady
47	Safari on Mors Island
54	A Journey in 1944
60	Fragments of a Mirror
65	A Man and His Great-Grandfather
71	The Horse on the Beach
77	Sleep
81	The Weeping Beech
89	The Specter of Regret
95	Thirty Years Later
100	Vanished Summers
105	September 1939
110	A Hunting Trip
115	Inuit Nuna
121	The Window Ajar
126	The Wind in West Jutland

Preface

The sun had gone down. My wife Jette and I pulled up in our tiny rental car to massive iron gates at the end of a narrow dead-end Danish street. Maybe we had lingered a bit too long at our visit with Benny Andersen in Copenhagen, but he and his wife Elisabeth are such lovely company. Now we had driven just north of the city for our only chance on this trip to visit Tårbæk Church, where Knud Sønderby was supposedly buried in the churchyard. It has always been important to me to make a personal connection to an author I was translating. Hence the visit with Benny Andersen. But Sønderby had been dead nearly 50 years. I wanted at least to visit his grave, and I had dragged my wife along with me.

The wrought iron gates were unlocked. We slipped through them onto the quiet church grounds. The historic stone building with it's steep roof rose stark and tall against the darkening blue sky. The far wall of the church was bordered by the graveyard, consisting of long rows of upright stones of varying sizes on plots separated by low bushes, tiny fences, or sections of metal chain. We wondered if we could find his grave before it got too dark.

I had anticipated that an accomplished author such as Sønderby would have a large stone, one that was easy to find, perhaps adorned with birds or gilded angels. We got up close to each stone to read the names in the low light—Jensen; Olsen; Møller—finally ending at the edge of the cemetery where a fence separated it from the Deer Park, a favorite site for Sønderby. Jette and I made our way along the paths to the last row, to the end of the plots, and there was no Sønderby. And now it was dark.

I was wondering if perhaps we had somehow missed a section. Then we noticed a light on at an outbuilding near the church. And in the glow of that light a man was standing, talking on a cellphone. Who goes to cemeteries at night? I approached him slowly, and after he hung up I excused myself as an American tourist looking for a particular grave. Would he know anything about where Knud Sønderby was buried? He'd never heard of him and he had no idea. But his wife was the director of the cemetery and he would call her for me.

We stood in the silent churchyard, in the dim light outside the public restroom, while he listened to his wife's response. He relayed to me that she wasn't sure, but she thought that his grave might be in the "urn yard," and he pointed to a huge swath of lawn across from the church door. On the lawn were hundreds of smallish, rounded stones with engraved names. We thanked him and walked over to the burial ground. My wife said, "There's no way we're going to find it by looking at each one. There's too many and it's too dark. Let's just follow our intuitions." We opened our cell phones for light. She walked straight ahead and slightly left, shining her phone on stones along the way; I walked further to the left, bent over, reading names.

I was having no luck. Then I looked up. Ten yards ahead, Jette was standing with her arm outstretched, slowly waving her cellphone light. "You found it?" I said. I hurried over. She stood by a rounded oval stone, engraved with Sønderby's name above his wife's. I knelt down and had a moment of prayer with Sønderby, thanking him for his contribution to this world—a collection of beautiful writing which has been a valuable gift to me and to many others.

Then I noticed that on this vast lawn, otherwise devoid of landscaping, a medium-sized tree was growing just behind Sønderby's stone. I thought it might be a hawthorn, since that was the title of one of his essay collections—and it was. I knew for sure when I reached out for it, because it stuck me painfully on my hand. I had forgotten that hawthorns are covered with long, needle-like thorns all over their bark. I took out the Danish-American flag pin that I had brought with me to leave on his grave. There was no flat surface anywhere on which to leave it. Carefully I stuck it in the crotch of the tree. Maybe it's still there.

Michael Goldman
Florence, Massachusetts, USA
September, 2016

Translator's Introduction

Knud Sønderby is a master of observation. In his essays he presents us with the woman in a tent of silver fox attacking her way through the train with her hatboxes. And the girl who coaxes the author to risk life and limb in the woods, as he follows her on horseback. And the Greenlandic boy who displays the traits of a fierce hunter before even being old enough to wipe his own nose. And the man-of-the-world ferry passenger, lulled to sleep by the drone of the ship, who burrows his way into a pile of tarpaulins so the only trace of him left is a pushed-up trouser leg and a purple sock garter.

Sønderby asks, with half a smile, why are we here if not to observe with all our faculties the novelty of life? After decades of driving in cars, he discovers that riding on his bicycle seems like pedaling a steamroller. In another essay he asks why, if darkness is the most fundamental of all things, do we forsake and fear it? Always in his prose there is a perpetual undercurrent of the multitudinousness that life presents—what he calls "a dazzling mastery in immutability."

Sønderby's writing is also inescapably Danish. His observations are made wholly within a Danish context—the ferries, the wind, the rural and urban landscapes and people. But while the details may be specific to the Danish experience, there is a universality to the emotional undercurrent. When reading his essays, you may have the experience of sensing a Danishness within yourself that you never before knew was there.

Knud Sønderby wrote as a journalist for major Danish newspapers in the 1930s and 40s while also translating numerous works into Danish for the Royal Theater. He later published four novels, two plays, and six essay collections. When he died in 1966, three of his essays were translated into English and published in a thin commemorative volume. Two of those essays appear here, in all-new translations, in addition to twenty other selected essays which show Sønderby at the height of his craft. Fifty years after his death, I am pleased to share this collection with English-language readers.

Fragments of a Mirror

Addiction to speed

Sometimes I experience things that make the term *speed* rattle around inside of me like something baffling. The riddle disappears in the intangible, but the question mark remains hanging like smoke after a locomotive.

I have a friend, for example. I have noticed that when we are out driving, and for one reason or another we have to stop for a moment, it makes him very uncomfortable. And he's no teenager or biker; he has driven a car every day for half a lifetime. Speed, sitting behind the wheel and being in control are nothing new and miraculous to him.

But when the kids start yelling for ice cream or hot dogs, he says, "Okay, okay, sure, fine, I'll stop when we see one."

And when they yell enthusiastically, "Dad, There's one! There's an ice cream man! There's a hot dog cart! Dad! Dad!" he speeds right by.

And when they complain that, "There was one right there!" and, "You promised!" he sits there with his hands on the wheel staring far out ahead and says, "Yes, but now we've passed it, and I'll stop at the next one." And landscapes and hot dog carts and ice cream stands whiz by, and when he finally gives in to the combined family pressure of cries and protests, he says, "Okay, take it easy," as if irritated and slightly amazed at the commotion, as if he'd never had the least bit against stopping and taking a break whenever and wherever—"For god's sake, can't you see, I pulled over!"

And while they swarm out of the car, he remains sitting, nervously drumming with his fingers on the steering wheel, moving around uncomfortably in his seat, while cars that he passed long ago now pass him and get in front again. He sighs resignedly as if something or other is now completely in vain. He groans from time to time as if in actual physical pain—all this even though he's not in a rush at all, and even though they might be absolutely necessary stops.

Once we stopped outside a bakery half a mile from the vacation house which was the goal of our trip. We were actually at our destination, had a whole day ahead of us, and the bread was needed for lunch. He tried to control himself, but while a fresh bread was being put into a bag, complaints worked their way out of his tortured breast, like a moan from a stagnating martyrdom.

And there I sat beside him, tactfully silent with my wondering: *What is he suffering from? From where does his trouble originate? What in the world is it?*

And at the same time you know all about it already. It's just that his reactions are especially acute. You know it from yourself. The irritation from having to stop. Speed creates stress and impatience about everything, as if speed were a goal in itself. It has many manifestations. After you have driven sixty miles per hour for a while and then you adjust to a speed limit sign of forty, you think you're moving at a snail's pace. To really verify it, try twenty-five miles per hour, now shaking your head. It's like standing still. Are they joking? You're out driving and come to a lovely place. Why don't you stop? And if you are stopped, why not stay there? But onward, onward.

As if by an invisible umbilical cord the car person can be tied to his restlessness, his speed, his vehicle. If he stops someplace in the landscape with the goal of taking a walk, the unconscious goal for the trip is returning to the car, continuing on. He walks with an uneasiness inside him, like a chain smoker who has said to himself: *Now I am not going to light a cigarette for the next hour.* And when he reaches the car again, he is relieved. You know that look car owners get when they emerge from the roadside bar or from the roadside, where the card table was set with coffee cups at the forest's edge, the expression when they insert the key in the car door: security, delight, home again.

Speed is really very strange. And also dangerous. Speed takes hold of you and does not release you willingly.

You recognize it when you have to answer the call of nature, yet still you postpone it mile after mile, minute after minute, agonizing minutes and miles of well-suited stretches of road whizzing by. Just one more rise and then the next stretch of road and one more rise. For goodness sakes, it's as if you're hunting something that will get away if you apply the brakes.

And you slow down, stop the motor, open the door, go behind the car and stand at the roadside weeds, and suddenly it is as if reality has taken on a new dimension. The landscape surrounds you, pulls you close, creeps towards you from all sides, silently, hushed, keeps coming, brushes against you, tries to make itself understood. Sometimes it might flinch, pull back like from the lash of a whip when another car speeds by, but then it returns to you again, a mute animal—the growing silence. The lack of speed rivets you to the spot—and to something inside yourself. These particular blades of grass, this palpable bush, which just *is* and is *here*....

And then into the car and off again—like the devil's on your heels, like you've escaped from something.

And maybe that is precisely what has happened. Maybe this is precisely the secret of speed, speed's seduction, what it offers you. You escape from something.

We speak about the intoxication of speed, and we mean a certain devil-may-care exhilaration, in which the danger factor contributes an essential element.

But the word also has meaning from another point of view.

The pleasant effect of a narcotic is that it liberates you from reality, at any rate from reality's most intimate relations. Things appear immensely entertaining, but as if at a distance, so you could not care less. Speed also creates distance, pushes things away, loosens our engagement. When you are speeding along in a car or in a train, your gaze is naturally focussed out in the distance, out towards the horizon, towards objects which, in contrast to your own speed, are relatively at rest. What is nearby whizzes quickly behind you—the eye can't focus on it. You remember your preoccupation the first times you rode on a train as a child—almost the best part was the banks of grass by the railroad that flattened out, flickered, and were made surreal by speed. You didn't have time to focus; you couldn't see what was closest to you! A once-in-a-lifetime experience—you learned to adjust your focus. Coincidentally, the same natural staring at the close by, the same shocking experience of not being able to see it anymore—this experience was also shared by Hans Christian Andersen when he, as an adult, rode on a train for the first time. He wrote about it. It was remarkable. You are compelled to focus your gaze farther away.

The intoxication of speed. Like a partial removal of consciousness. You push things away, see like the intoxicated see; nothing really reaches you.

But, it must also be said, we do get around. Car, train, plane. We tear around for hours, days, look and look, since we are looking the whole time. But what we remember most clearly are always the times we weren't moving—the times the car stopped, the train stopped, the times that things and events were able to reach us. At high speed we do of course take in and remember things—that some places there were mountains, other places high plains, some places it was different than at home. The soil could have another color, the houses be built in another way, etc. But this fades away from memory, plays no role in relation to the times we stayed in one place. *They* exist, they live in our memories, they show up.

I remember the three scraggly chickens in a country road mechanic's garden better than all the hideous mountains on Napoleon's Route combined. And that place where I bought cigarettes and oranges and the coincidental place where I stopped for ten minutes by the side of the road and took out the jack and changed a tire—those places, those minutes I remember more clearly. They occupy more room, are more alive in my memory, than the whole remainder of the trip over the Apennines, Passo del Bracco, the trip over the Bracco pass—something with huge green mountainsides. But the restaurant on the top! The tiny comical cafeteria where a dashing restauranteur with a Clark Gable mustache wanted 1000 lire for a laughable slice of coffee cake. In plastic! With raisins! I can still see that plastic swindle: the man standing there affectedly, believing that the whole world were idiots and that he was so incredibly smart. Oh, then there was something else about the hospitality as soon as I crossed over the French border on the outward journey, where I wanted to enjoy my first Amer Picon—absolutely sacred, just one, just stop for a minute. And three weeks later, when I was on the return trip, they remembered me, just as I had remembered them and the inn: *Ah monsieur, it was you, who forgot your hat.* It was there! It *was* there, I had left it. But what do I remember from the trip, from the drive to it or from it. I arrived at an inn. Then I left the inn. Then I came back to it again. I arrived. I arrived. We don't remember coming, not the word in its geographical length—it was a disappearing act, it went by too fast. From travelogues you always read *we arrived* as if what lay between, the stretches that were traveled, played no role at all. We remember in points, we remember in moments, we remember in stillness. Speed causes the points to blur, prevents the moment from sinking in, the stillness from growing.

You fly or ride on a train for hours or days, and the landscape's diversity—mountains, lakes and valleys—are remembered only remotely, like something you observed with your back turned, like something that took place behind you, even though you stared out the window mile after mile. But the toilet, that you remember, that you will never forget—though you were there as briefly as possible and took in as little as you could. The old lady with the rosary beads that you passed in the hall, and the married couple next to you who ate food they had packed: they also have imprinted themselves, even though you tactfully did not stare.

Perhaps the human eye, the human consciousness, only earnestly takes in with true intensity things that are near to us. Perhaps the potential for the outside world's being imprinted on us is inversely proportional to the distance of things from us. And stillness creates nearness, while speed creates distance. The eye cannot perceive the close by when we are moving fast. And what is close by makes the greatest impression. Only what is close by is truly alive to us.

From a Sunday drive I took with some friends, I remember only a particular ice cream stand that children swarmed around, and a country bakery with the traditional knotted pastry sign hanging in the air, and milk crates on the ground. And my friend, who sat drumming on the steering wheel making half-choked sounds while I was inside. An addict's martyrish abstinence symptoms.

I've never done much walking; that was before my time. I was raised with the bicycle.

One day when I was without other modes of transportation, I dug out my bicycle from its archeological sleep behind layers of discarded recliners and junk, got it out—a curiosity—into the daylight, pumped it up and swung myself up on it, as they say. I sat once again on a bicycle, held once more a steering wheel, curiously. And I pedaled, pedaled and pedaled, and regardless of how hard I pedaled, it was as if the ground, as if this Jylland back road, stood still beneath me. Was something wrong? Did it need lubrication? Did I put enough air in the tires? I couldn't get it going, even though I worked until the sweat poured off of me.

So I gave up and collapsed panting back on the seat. I was exhausted. This was no bicycle; it was a steamroller! And while I coasted, out of breath, the strangest thing happened. The bicycle didn't stop, it just slowed down. Suddenly I was riding a bicycle like a bicycle was meant to be ridden, in the proper tempo. I recognized this, sank relaxed back to days that had disappeared long ago when everything was different, when things fit, happened at exactly this speed, in this rhythm, and when there was nothing wrong with it; when it was, on the contrary, completely natural. It was not the bicycle that something had been wrong with, it had been my own sense of time, my own life rhythm. There was nothing wrong with my leg muscles and my heart—it was my impatience.

Now everything came streaming around me and past me and inside me—sky and earth and road and landscape—not in an incessant escape, but in a continual meeting. The things were there and I was among them. No need to rush. That is how it is, when you allow yourself a little time.

Slowly I wheeled off in a vanished bliss. Everything touched me, congregated heart-warmingly around me, but still was sadly distant. Recognition and yet complete foreignness. I felt what I had lost, sensed at the same time that, despite my recognition, it was lost for ever. I could bike until doomsday, but never bike in the same natural ease, the same natural tempo. Like something precious and remarkable I could recognize the naturalness; ill at ease I could still identify with the total composure.

And every time afterwards when I have ridden my bicycle, I have had the same feeling of something lost, a lost rhythm, a lost way of life.

How addicted have I become? Am I a hopeless case? Is it the case that once you have been intoxicated by speed that you never again will be able to have the same peace in your soul without it?

Have we, in just a couple of generations, become foreign to millennia of our predecessors? Has speed caused a mutation in our sense of living?

Who will be able to walk like Blicher and Holberg walked? Like all of them who *walked*?

You sense a peace, a nearness, a familiarity with the surroundings, a gaze directed towards but not past.

We have a half-forgotten term in our language; now only a curiosity. It encapsulates what is for us an unknown intimacy: the word *wayfarer*.

*   *   *

Translator's Note: Steen Steensen Blicher (1782—1848) was a pioneer of the short story and regional writing in Denmark. He was known particularly for his depictions of rural life and his walks on the heathlands in Jutland. Ludvig Holberg, Baron of Holberg (1684—1754) was a playwright, historian, essayist, and philosopher. He was born in Bergen, Norway, but spent most of his adult life in Denmark.

The Black Swan

Red at the bottom, a green stripe, and black otherwise, it stands in front of my house and I work on it: The Black Swan. I own a dinghy. I'm a boat owner—ship operator, almost.

A boat like this needs a lot of maintenance. Sal-ammoniac, sandpaper, putty, paint, varnish—but it is enjoyable work and it looks decorative standing there in the field with the fjord in the background. I have hung an eel trap on the side for extra maritime effect and I am speculating about eventually acquiring a discreet tattoo. I am not sure I have the heart to set the boat in the water.

To begin with I was not so excited about it. I got it through my cousin. My desire to have a boat had been purely abstract, of the type that it was natural of course to have a boat when one lives by a fjord and has the convenience of being able to set it in the water anytime and go for a trip. It was effortless in thought. When you think about setting a boat in the water, you do it with one hand, with two fingers on one hand. The process takes no length of time, is over and done with in the time it takes to smile a toothpaste grin.

Of course it would be nice to have a boat at some point. I said as much, in a non-committal tone, and it was already like sailing a bit. I had said it to my cousin, an old sailor who had sailed with sailboats: *It would be nice to have a boat someday.* To say it to him was like going further out to sea, sailing the seven seas, and it excited me. And he took me at my word and came back with a deal—a dinghy with sail and outboard motor, and guaranteed as a tradesman the whole thing, including the price's incomparable reasonableness. He stood there, enthusiastic on my behalf, for here was just the thing I had wanted. He'd been looking at boats for me for months, and here, finally, was the perfect one. It just had to be sent by train from one side of the country to the other, but he would take care of that, and all the practical details—something about train stations, dispatchers, homeward sailing, mooring place, etc. He would help with all of it, of course.

The puzzlement of a wish's fulfillment. The discomfort of a wish's fulfillment.

I felt like when I was a little boy and I finally got bunnies. The reality takes you by surprise. Suddenly there it is, standing there with its scythe of responsibility, its cage of duties. You have been taken at your word.

I lived up to the excitement to the best of my ability, to a happy expectancy anyway. And when the time finally arrived I followed along with him to my house from across the country, and I inwardly thought that that was plenty for one day. Pouring rain, the windshield wipers whistling and hissing in my face for hours, spray and splashing from other cars. And we arrived at the place and I thought that anything to do with a boat could definitely wait for another day; but no, for some reason it couldn't be postponed. There were many things lined up, and the harbormaster was waiting.

I surrendered, took my feet out of the stirrups, released myself from responsibility for myself and my life, let him do with me whatever he wanted, followed along with a resigned inward head-shaking. To town to get a rope of a particular kind. Of course we'll go to town to get a rope. Evidently we don't need food, I didn't think so, just a hot dog from a hot dog cart— that's so quaint anyway. And then a search for a couple of fishing weirs to make it fast with. Did I hear him right? Fishing weirs! Sure, why not, why don't we in God's name search the country high and low for fishing weirs. And while we're at it, how about a few other small items since I probably don't have anything else to fill my time with, or so think some certain individuals. And these fishing weirs have to be hammered in at the ocean's edge, and it has to happen today. By all means! He must be out of his mind, that now just the two of us will carry these nine-foot long, heavy fishing weirs down to the beach, and stand in the wind with waves up to our waists and pound them in. Or maybe one of us will have to stand under the water, with the other one on his shoulders, and the one on the bottom will be me, of course. Just by happening, in an innocent non-committal way, to breathe the word boat, people come and pursue you with tonnage, turn your existence inside out with their cursed vessels. Can't you be left in peace? Can't you open your mouth? I wish that boat and everything that belongs with it were sent to Bloksbjerg.

And then you have to be careful not to form too obvious a contrast to his zeal and stamina, fight back your taciturnity and impatience, act satisfied when he does, excited when he sees occasion for it. Fate controlled me, came rolling in from far away. I had released it myself and I knew it.

The day's celebratory finale consisted of driving to the town where the boat sat waiting at a railroad station. This summerly town, that I otherwise enjoy, was transformed into a depressing railroad site, damp shipping papers, gloomy sheds and desolate wharfs, hour after hour; and my self reduced to tramping idiotically on the heels of station workers, harbormasters and dispatchers, tuned out like a four-year-old child, when grown men have serious business to attend to. I tried at least to help with the lifting, but there wasn't even room for me there— *watch out, stand to the side* —; now they're going to lift the boat down from the flatbed, six men in the rain who know what they're doing, and—*watch out, move over*—; now they are setting it in the sluice and into the water with it. I stood still, arms hanging, just staring.

So there it floated, rocking in the rain and the coming twilight. It actually did *that*, too. It was something of a shock for me since I had figured, in my sluggish, steamrolled state, that we were about done with that boat, and now we could finally put it away, escape the sight of it. Just a few bubbles and ripples left behind and down to the ocean bottom forever, so I could be myself again, turn around and go into town, which also could become itself again, just like everything else, finally. But there it floated, rocking, ready for anything, high in the water, bobbing coquettishly with my inadequacy, my powerlessness and my flight response intact on board.

The next day we would, of course, sail it homeward.

It floated there still—this time in full daylight—but it had changed its appearance somewhat. It rocked gently at the end of the slack line, had calmed down, with an atmosphere of having resigned itself to its fate. Just the fact that it still floated there created the impression of something loyal and deeply touching. But I wasn't so touched that I couldn't immediately, relieved, enter into a division of labor, where I had to do the shopping while he rigged the mast and set the motor.

Break-time. In my summer town. In a delicatessen I bought a tray of sandwiches and in a market a couple of beers, and that didn't take long. And since it was Saturday, when there could have been a lot of people in the shops, I had time to spare. So I went into a pub and let the pause descend blessedly over me. I relaxed after all the maritime trouble, extended the time as long as possible, sent a prayer to the sailors and understood, that after a turbulent existence they sought relief in the nearest public house, seeking oblivion in the bottle. On the way back to the harbor there was another pub, but I resisted it.

He took it very well, just smiled and asked why I hadn't invited him. I regretted it, too. I suggested that we go do it now, but he wouldn't think of it. Of course.

We stowed the baggage, and then the great moment arrived when we would start the outboard motor. He was nervous, on my behalf, that it wouldn't start; and I was nervous on his behalf, because he was nervous on my behalf. The whole thing was magnified because people were standing watching, hands in their pockets, and he thought that because of this, I would feel embarrassed. Teeth clenched, he pulled the rope a couple of times, and the motor started and I felt a great relief on his behalf. The first few minutes that we sailed out of the harbor he sat completely still from the passing excitement, had to slowly recover. Silently we saw the wharfs get smaller and smaller and the Limfjord's banks broadened before us, first over the broad bay at Thisted, and past there through the narrow Vil Sound and out past more wide bays. It was several hour's sailing we had before us, but on the other side was the final leg, and a certain sense of well-being blossomed inside me— one final leg before the boat could be fixed at its mooring, responsibly tied, and I could escape from concerning myself with it any further. To pass the time I started assembling a fishing rig, so I could let a trout lure drift behind the boat, but he counteracted me. Willingly enough, he slowed the motor to a suitable speed, but when he thought I wasn't paying attention, he slowly, carefully increased the speed again, did it several times, wasn't interested in our fishing, didn't believe in it. Of course I could have shouted, said: For God's sake, slow it down and keep it there! I could have used the opportunity to let off steam, it would have been perfectly fine. But I couldn't be bothered; I didn't have enough interest in the enterprise myself.

"Don't you want to fish anymore?" he asked in shameless wonder, when I packed away the fishing gear. I shook my head. Instead I unpacked our lunch. This he didn't have anything against. No sabotage there.

Vil Sound Bridge was something of a shock to me. I was sure that, of course, we would just sail right under it with the mast and everything, while he expressed doubt.

"So what do you think?" he asked when we were a hundred yards away, and I had to admit to myself, that the bridge was lower than I had thought.

"It's fine," I said stubbornly.

"Well, now what do you think?" he asked, when we were fifty yards away. I nodded and sat ready to jump. It looks scary under a bridge like that: dark and sinister above and black water below.

"You're the skipper," he said and kept sailing. Then I gave a cry of panic and jumped to my feet. He reversed the motor, while I got the mast lowered.

"Thank the good Lord," I said, when we sailed through the darkness under colossal steel beams. I lowered my head.

"Told you so," he said, laughing.

We had to relax after the excitement. We tied up the boat by a little swaying bridge in Vil Sound and went ashore there. It was a strange feeling walking along, knowing that the dinghy lay tied with fine half-hitches to certain bollards, waiting for us; to walk down the bridge and not turn around, still knowing it the whole time. We walked up to a shop, and I said it was no use, that it would be closed at this hour. But he said of course they'll be open, and he bought us a couple of beers which we drank, sitting on the shop's back patio. Then I went in with the bottles, and the shopkeeper asked if we wanted a couple more for the other leg. I agreed to his offer, and brought them out as if I had done a good deed. We sat in the plastic chairs smoking cigarettes and enjoying ourselves. Then he went in with the bottles and said that there was a problem, because the second beer had gone down the same leg. I didn't want any more; I felt a sense of responsibility for the boat and the trip and besides that, I owed him money.

"You can go down and get the boat ready in the meantime," he said. So I did. I knew the real reason he said it, but I did it anyway, let him stay behind in his plastic chair and went down across the fishing village and over the swaying bridge and down into the boat and felt like I had come home again. He had said it so I could be alone with the boat, become intimate with it, like you would say to a little child: Go ahead and pet it, go over to the dog and pet it—it won't hurt you. But I didn't care; I wanted to go ahead down to the boat. I sat puttering around, lifted some floorboards and bailed out the bit of water that had collected, checked that the mast was properly lashed, and prepared the motor.

When he arrived I was ready. We shoved off and I took over the steering, pulled the motor, and it started immediately. Then we continued sailing gently through the narrow Vil Sound, where there was shelter and completely smooth water, and the sun was shining. It was beautiful in this narrow passage with soft banks on both sides. One place we stopped the motor and drifted, watching a couple of boys, also out in a boat, who were tending to an eel trap. We leaned over the railing and watched as the last of the eel trap finally surfaced. There were several good eels in it. We were just as excited as the boys and had a nice talk with them. But when we asked if we could buy a couple of eels, they became suspicious and reticent—they weren't selling any eels.

They rowed to shore with their catch, and we used the opportunity now, while the motor was stopped anyway, to row close in to land, hop overboard, and have a swim. When we were sailing again, my cousin lay down in the bottom of the boat with a cushion under his head and closed his eyes, just enjoying himself. I was certain that he did this mainly to demonstrate to me what a great time I could have in my boat.

After Vil Sound, when we emerged where the fjord again was over two miles wide on all sides, we decided to take a detour. We sailed east. We made landfall on Mors. You can do things like this when you have a boat—are a boat owner. You can sail around and go in to land whenever you want. It's really irresistible—you just sail along as far as you want, cast anchor, hop overboard in the warm shallow water, wade in, and tread the new ground of the island. We walked up through the streets of the town. The whole time we walked I had in the back of my mind a picture of the boat as it lay rocking out in the shallow fjord. A bakery was open, and we walked in and bought two popsicles. For no real reason I bought a loaf of fresh bread as well, though he protested and said that we had lots of bread at home, and I knew he was right. But I just felt that since we were in a bakery, it was only natural to buy a bread, and afterwards natural and fitting to walk around with it under my arm. So we walked around a bit, like you do when you have just made landfall from a boat, are guests on land, on solid ground—footloose guests. Outside the church walls we sat on a bench, ate our popsicles and studied the Mors-ites, and laughed at them a bit, without however being able to draw any final conclusions—the examples were too few.

But we had to see about pushing on, see about getting on board, quite easily, out through the shallow water, up into the boat, in with the anchor, pull the motor, out into the wide world, out over the wide fjord where we could barely spy land on the other side. I sat in a particularly excited triumphant mood, and suddenly I realized why I had bought bread. Completely unconsciously I had had an intention. It was so it could be just like this. Now something was happening! I had freight on board. I was sailing a loaf of fresh bread from Mors to Thy!

I hope that he didn't see through it. I don't think so. And yet. Is there anything at all that people don't perceive about one another, or at least sense?

"Well, what do you think?" he asked once, when we were midway out in the fjord, far to land on all sides, everything just water while we sat up on our little dinghy. "Isn't this nice?"

I nodded. Didn't have to say anything.

"Can't you see it was good we got everything ready yesterday, even though you were in a bit of a bad mood?" he continued.

I denied that I had been in a bad mood. I wasn't in a bad mood at all. I was thunderstruck that he could have thought that.

"That we don't have to start the day today by getting the boat from the railroad and that we don't have to pound in the weirs when we get back, but that everything is already done?" he continued.

Of course, I knew that all along. And I wasn't in a bad mood. A bit inconvenienced, perhaps. I had other things to think about, of course. I was sorry he got that impression.

He nodded. Didn't have to say anything. I had acknowledged the accuracy of his arrangements. There was a clean slate, no bitterness.

As if we could just as well be starting over, he asked me to stop the motor. Silently but determined, he prepared the anchor, threw it overboard, and when he felt it grab the bottom, tied off the line to the bow.

"Now you have to get to know your motor," he said.

"Oh crap, just when things were going so well," I groaned aloud. "Can't that wait until tomorrow? Let's wait until we get in to shore!"

"Nope, you have to learn how to deal with it while you're out in the boat. Situations can arise when you're all alone—dangerous situations—and there's no one but you. So you have to be able to deal with it."

He looked at me somberly with a screwdriver in his hand.

"Fine," I said resignedly. Let him, I thought. He is so damned sweet. He has been so great. I really like him. A few seconds later he was kneeling on the stern thwart with his rear in the air and hex keys in his hands. He took apart the whole works and gave a lecture, hiding his excitement behind a serious expression. Every time he turned his head and lectured I craned my neck and looked interested. The only bright spot was a spark plug. I understood some of it, but wasn't sure where he put it in the end. But he enjoyed it. And he was right. Eternally right. It was just that if something really did happen, a situation, etc., I would, without running the smallest risk of shifting course, immediately curse the motor, pray to God, and start rowing. You won't find me in a windstorm on my knees on the stern thwart, with my rear in the air and my head on the water's surface in the trough of a wave, playing the little engineer.

When it was over, and the motor didn't sound like it had been harmed at all, he relaxed again. He sat there splicing various lines, securing the ends very nicely. "Then they won't unravel on you," he said. "And it looks pretty, doesn't it?"

In this I could follow him. It did look pretty, nice to hold in your hand. There is nothing like rope, or any kind of ship parts. A splice like that, that kind of mending can tell you more than a whole historical or maritime museum. I thought for a second that it was that kind of thing that architects would call exquisite, a *good* thing; and then why should *they* now come running in and destroy my sense of it. But then I forgot them again because it was so pretty and clever and so genuine to touch—honest, good—no funny business there; it was from before the time of funny business.

We had been sitting preoccupied with our heads together like two boy scouts.

While I walk around now and look at the boat, and sometimes paint it, I can't help but think about the trip we had back then. It is as if *that* is what I am staring at while I searchingly observe the painted boards, *that* which I am looking back on while I cast my vision out over the fjord.

"Hey, you've got a good boat here," he said once. "And this is a terrific place to sail...I think you are going to be happy with it. I'm happy for you. And it is a beautiful place to sail."

"I think so too," I said. I sure was happy with it already. I had been the whole time. Really happy.

That conversation we could have had ten years ago, twenty, thirty, forty years ago.

There we sat in my little dinghy and the moments were like they always had been when we were together. We just sat there and he was just my cousin like he always had been.

Cape Horn. A couple of sentences I remember he once had said at another occasion:

"Cape Horn. Sometimes it's strange to think about. I have been there several times—around Cape Horn. Now that sailing route is desolate, abandoned. No ships sail there any more."

Another time, as a sailor during World War I, he sat out on the yard and saw a torpedo coming:

"A second later I stood clutching the mast without knowing how I had gotten there. I god-damned ran over the yard. Like a tightrope walker. I have no idea how."

There he sat, had sailed the seven seas. And none of us gave it a second thought. That sailing trip we were on could just as well have been ten, twenty, thirty, forty years ago.

When he lay down in the bottom of the dinghy, lay there rocking with a cushion under his head, so I could see how great it could be, he was a fat old man. But even though I saw it, even though I was there in the boat, I had to consciously call forth the impression, imprint it like a stamp: fat, old. Because he was not old and I was not old—we were like we always had been. And yet we were as old as our grandfather was. And he was very old.

When we suddenly climbed overboard and into the water at the narrow Vil Sound. When we sat on the bench in front of the church on Mors: old, fat men.

We were men in our mid-fifties and mid-sixties and neither of us gave it a second thought. The pattern between us was unchanged. We were like we always had been. Nothing had changed. We were the age we always had been, that indistinct age between 15 and 30, that age you stay stuck in, while the body goes its own way.

*   *   *

Translator's note: Bloksbjerg is the fanciful destination of witches burned in effigy on bonfires during traditional midsummer celebrations in Denmark. It is also a mountain in Germany.

Deer Park in the Dark

On one of the other benches an old man sat looking out over the Hermitage grounds. Besides that there was nothing but night and solitude. I couldn't see him, could barely tell if he was even a person. He sat in the dark in front of the Hermitage balustrade, and it was mostly just a feeling that he was there and that he was an old man. I could hear that he sat with his cane between his feet, and when he coughed, I could hear that he sat mostly with his head back looking upward. And it occurred to me then, that at night you look up much more than during the day.

Just above us there were slight fluted clouds illuminated by the moonlight, and sometimes there were peepholes to a night sky much, much higher. But otherwise on the horizon all around loomed only heavy threatening cloud cover. The clouds reached up over the sky, flowing into it with darkness further below and locking us in a dome of night and stillness and sensations of drowning, for it looked like rain. The moon shone over the road to Peter Liep's Inn and fought its way in a tough-sailing biting wind through the clouds, swung and cut its way diagonally downward, fought its way from one peephole to another. And turning my gaze forward, I saw that the stand of trees by Deer Creek Road looked like a huge supernatural creature rolled over to rest by the roadside, huddled up and good-natured. I have a sense for friendly, good-natured things when it is dark. I can rest my eyes while imagining beneficence. The terrible creature had rolled over on its side; it wouldn't hurt a thing. It was at peace, its large back arched as high as a house in the dark, and it had laid its tired head to rest in the field. It warmed my heart to have it lying there so untroubled by the onward-rolling cloud banks.

Whenever I am alone in the night I get an impression of its remarkable qualities. And this was no special or lyrical night. It was an everyday darkness, a random and completely unsung fall night; and it even looked like rain. But the dark has something festive about it, something cathedral-like, even when it is completely random. You bend over backwards in devotion, while time stands still, watchful and attentive toward the light and the life that is yet still present.

The old man on the other bench got himself together at last, rose and began to walk away over the gravel. "Goodnight," he said, because the dark had united us. I could hear how he sought to find his own voice for this farewell, how he tried to recall it from the night, like trying to remember an unfamiliar voice. In the end he just used one of the incidental voices with which the night had populated his throat, and for a long time after, this foreign voice sounded in his own ears just as in mine. He was erased near the trees and the grass—just a few strides away he was entirely disappeared—but I still could hear him. He turned down the road towards Springforbi. His footfall, as well as the sound of his cane tip hitting the stones, leaped back toward me. His walking persisted in the air, just by my ears, for many minutes. I heard him after he passed the first stand of trees; I heard him shift from the hard stones in the middle of the road to the edge where it was softer. With the sounds of his movements the night bound us together so intimately, as if it had a fateful intent. He crossed over the road to Red Bridge, maybe a kilometer away; only then did the sound of his footsteps finally disappear. But once he coughed sharply, like a final admonition.

Now suddenly it is entirely quiet over this field in Deer Park. The last crack in the coffin is sealed and I am alone in the dark. I know this place as well as I know the back of my hand. I know it the way you know things you have known from your childhood and were brought up with. "They've gone down Deer Creek Road!" I have yelled and thrown myself on my bicycle so my hair stood up like inverted stems of wheat. "The Fortune Inn!" resounded in my mind as I maneuvered my bicycle through a troublesome and temperamental red gate. These things are taken for granted in my mind. They have become a part of myself. Well-worn names are freed from their ornamental meanings. Three-Willow Gate was just Three-Willow Gate: a shout, a sound, a place. In my ear it had nothing to do with willow trees or their total number. It was all so self-evident, like the back of my hand.

But at night it all changes. Maybe because even you yourself change in the darkness. It is still the back of your own hand, as far as you know, but now the hand is attached to another man's arm.

Suddenly over by the golf courses there appears a doe. Sound is pouring out of her throat. A tender call like from a toy trumpet, ignored at any other time, but here in the night it takes on an enhanced existence, a magic meaning, spreads itself malleably over the entire grounds. It rises out of the darkness, and in the darkness it dwells. You follow the sound, as if it were a frightened bird taking wing in order to escape. And not until the last weak reverberations have hidden themselves, to rest again in a grass tuft high up by Miller's River, are you able to pull your attention free from it.

Apart from the moon's wrestling up in the plaited clouds, you are left only with what you can barely hear. And then you jump. The White Lady! The rumored specter of a tormented noblewoman! You catch a glimpse of her to the left, out of the corner of your eye, quickly, but distinctly! You stare rigidly forward. You know that it cannot be a White Lady, absolutely not. Your parents and your teachers promised you. When you look around again, it will probably reveal itself to have been a wild animal or a piece of paper lifted up by a gust of wind. But you would like to know beforehand which of these....

So it was just the stone statue on the balustrade in a sudden illumination of the moon. But before the roots of your hair stand calmly down, there she is again, and this time for real, there is no question. The White Lady floating over the grounds up towards the mansion. But it turns out she is not alone. She is wearing a white jacket—only this emerges in the darkness over the grass. The rest of her, like the young man with whom she is walking, blends with the background. They walk toward me, but a discreet coughing fit causes them to veer away, and they sit on a bench on the other side of the stairs.

They have only gotten to know one another recently. The night carries their conversation, and by the tone it is evident that they are not using the familiar pronoun form, even though they haven't addressed one another. Their high-pitched courteous tones reveal this. But they are talkative; they are trying hard. It will not be long before they switch to the familiar. Besides their tone of voice, the topics of conversation also reveal their stages of getting acquainted. A couple of times she relates small bits from her childhood, what Father said, and what Grand-mom said, and summer vacations in the country as a child. Her voice is very light and animated, sometimes it is about to dissociate from her completely. He too relates a childhood memory, and they both laugh together, eagerly taking the happy opportunity. When two people speak about their childhood in that way, it's only a matter of time. They have discovered what a wonder the other one is, and how much they have in common. Every sentence wins ground for the harmonizing, and every electrifying silence is a basis from which new advances shall occur. As a little girl she often stayed with her uncle in Jylland during vacations. Now he shakes his head and smiles overwhelmed somewhere, there out in the darkness. He almost can't stand it. A completely amazing idyll is being handed to him. How is he deserving of this? She…as a lille girl… on vacation in Jylland…and she has an uncle just like regular mortals and doesn't even try to hide it. That's how unsnobbish she is. Entirely incomprehensible perspectives of bliss open up to him. Maybe she has even more family. A grandmother or a couple of little cousins. It would be unbearable. Nature's strange gentle jokes in connection with her would obliterate him. Everything she says makes a huge impression on him. And she sees what an impact it makes. She has never experienced a sensibility like his. Let's fall in love—before we get hysterical.

They disappear again into the darkness. I can hear that she has to jump over a ditch somewhere. I guess, that he reaches out for her. When she makes it over, she laughs aloud as a nervous release. He did reach out for her, you could hear it. They stood hand in hand when she laughed.

A little while later Deer Park is deserted again.

This strange condition we call darkness. The eyes can have a good rest by observing it. The face can unwrinkle, completely free of stress, to just receive the gentle breezes as a confidence, a friendly whispering word from the trees and the grass moved by the same wind. Just a friendly word or a stroke on the forehead, before you surrender yourself to the peace and solitude again.

Like a current of sound, the trotting of a horse from a carriage on Beach Road appears in my consciousness. It takes up quite a lot of room, and wants it all for itself. The horse is running heavy on its forelegs, as old horses do. All the way from Springforbi to Klampenborg its tired hoofbeats echo off the asphalt, almost moving in place, slowly embroidering an edge of sound around the nighttime park.

I start tapping out my pipe on the bench, but realize that it would be heard from Hjortekær to Tårbæk. Deer, lying in the grass from Fuglesang Lake to the Stampen Mill, would raise their heads, and with their large moveable ears take bearings on the sound from my pipe. Lovers would look away and maybe forget one another for a second, to listen. My eardrums would be shredded by the sound, because you become much more delicate and sacrosanct in the dark.

The extraordinary darkness, where everything seems to melt together and conceal itself. Ryegrass, cocksfoot, sedge and fescue. Beech trees, oak tress, birch and ash. In the dark they cover themselves. Things lose perspective. The night veils them. You can see farthest with your ears. Only sound has precision and creates concise perceptions of distance, when darkness hovers before your eyes.

Not only are things veiled by the night, but our usual perception of time can also be altered. The darkness builds its own perspective. There are oak trees in Deer Park that are about 900 years old. One of them is called the Deer Spring Oak, which stands in a clearing near the Kirstin Piils Spring. It has outlived an entire lineage of kings, was already an old oak under King Valdemar Sejr. During the day it feels strange, almost forced to try to think about this, but in the dark's gothic perspective it follows like a matter of course. Yet, even trees have a limited lifespan. And whatever has to do with time is erased completely except for the simplest concepts: the sound of treetops that suddenly are animated by a breeze under the night sky, then calm again; the sight of a moon that bravely fights its way over the clouds: these are things with age.

*   *   *

Translator's Note: Deer Park is a national park of 2700 acres, north of Copenhagen, originally fenced in by the Danish King Frederik III 350 years ago for royal hunting. Today it is a peaceful refuge characterized by protected forest, old buildings like the Hermitage and Peter Liep's Inn, a theater, grassy fields, and red portal gates like the one pictured on the book cover. Deer Park is also home to about 2000 deer.

Encounter with the Dark

One winter night in our house far out in the country the lights went out. A fuse must have blown. I realized this with a confused and lost feeling. I had had a book in my lap—still had it—a fraction of a second I could still remember it, see it before my eyes, see the whole living room with all its things and their relationship to one another the way it was in light. It was like the light still existed a moment after it went out. Then the darkness came.

I checked my pockets for a match, fumbled on the coffee table for them, but they weren't there, even though I knew they had to be.

So I sat for a few moments and just experienced the dark. Waited presumably for my eyes to adjust. But the dark simply got denser and denser, while my memory of light became weaker and weaker until it was like the very last candle on the Christmas tree, until it was like the very last ember on the wick of the very last candle. Then the dark came again—and came and came. And gradually I did, too —myself in darkness.

Matches. They had to be there. I felt around for them on the tabletop again.

This idea of eyes adjusting to the dark, I guess that only works when there's still a *little* light, at least not when it's completely dark.

Darkness is apparently even darker than we think. It's like—well, it's the darkest you can think of. It's something so dark that there aren't even any other words for it—it just *is*, is dark, black, beyond words, overshadowing synonyms, is the stuff that broods silently outside the illuminated purview of language, out there, where even words with panicked, rumbling, howling, and terrifying sounds can't describe it. Black, dark, noir, oscuro, gloom.

I fumbled around and found the matches, but only after knocking over my coffee. I lit the match and the coffee spilled across the table between books and papers which I just barely saved before the match went out and the dark washed over me again. So I went exploring to the kitchen, where I had a vague recollection of a candle somewhere. I found a stump of a candle and that was a big help; with its assistance I found one more. Now I could start to look around, look for new fuses—there weren't any—and for the flashlight—I had left it at a friend's house one evening when I was out visiting and had gotten a ride home. But still I had light—two islands of light—one in the kitchen and one in the living room. Just enough that I could recognize things and think about the situation—what in the world should I do?

The country store. Two miles away in rain and wind, and it might not even be open. The neighbors. I went out to the road to see if they were already in bed. Outside the door I fell over a bike that some goddamn idiot must have…oh yeah, that was me—it was my bike. But there were no lights on at the neighbor's—they must have been in bed—if I were even looking in the right direction.

Branches were knocking against each other in the wind over my head, but I couldn't see the tree. I couldn't see the road I was standing on, couldn't see the sky over the trees. There wasn't the faintest light to be seen anywhere, not even in the distance. I listened to the branches in the wind, and I got dizzy when I discovered that I couldn't see myself.

So I went inside again to the house's two tents of light. Strange, but it was like they were tents of silence, as if the darkness and silence went hand in hand. My otherwise very familiar furniture stood averted and unfamiliar in the ring of shadows, as if they had an issue left unresolved, like they had been given an apology but hadn't quite accepted it yet. You couldn't be sure that they wouldn't disappear completely. The cabinet, the pictures, the chairs; they were there, but for how long. They radiated silence, silence from another world towards which they were already turned, staying put for now, trapped by the little energy source on the table—how it worked hard, that quiet flame—giving of itself, burning itself up so things could exist, fighting for the life around it.

I tried to read, but couldn't concentrate, felt the light was too precious—not the stump of candle, but the *light*—too essential for me to occupy myself with anything but that, to think thoughts that didn't concern that. A book that wouldn't weaken the essential, a book that was about light and only light—that I could have read.

An encounter with the light—or maybe more correctly stated—with the dark, because isn't that the most elementary? Light in the darkness—it's complementary, of course. They exist only in relation to one another— in relation to us, at any rate.

A small accident with a highly complicated gadget must occur before a modern person suddenly discovers the most elemental of everything, notices it, feels it. You turn on three heaters instead of two, hit two switches without turning off a third; something with "so many watts," something with something in it so elemental in nature, yet utilized so complicatedly that you don't understand it, something like a fuse being overloaded—and then there you are! With the darkness making its presence felt again! Caught off-guard, exposed, attentive.

It's amazing how poorly the modern person knows the dark, so few times in our lives we have encountered it. From our childhood we remember a cellar, where we were sent down with the coal bucket in the evening, a switch that was worn out when flipped—we could just make it, running through the lit hallway. Then—if we were lucky—put the key in the padlock. We could, if we were very careful, maybe even open the door and enter the black cellar room while there was still light in the hall, so we could just barely see. It was important to make it as far as possible, important also because otherwise our song wouldn't last. Then it would happen. The light would go out. And we stood drowning to our core in darkness. And we sang, while we shoveled coal into the bucket, not loudly, but with clenched teeth, still singing—*Undaunted wherever you go…* our body like an organ of invocation—*Never fear the power of darkness…*Now we were already starting the second verse, and the bucket was only half full, and afterwards there was only one verse left—slower, sing slower, control our panic—don't squander the words, make them last!

And what was there to be afraid of? Just the darkness. Being separated from the world. Being alone and lost in this black unreality. Even though, as kids, we were in our own house, in a cellar hallway we knew inside and out, even though we knew our parents were right upstairs and they could hear us if we shouted—when the light went out we were the most alone individual in the world, forgotten and abandoned. It was like we stepped over the threshold to another world, where everything was changed, where lawlessness ruled over everything that we had always believed, knew, were sure of. A world so strange, so distant from the light that maybe our shouts couldn't be heard. Maybe we'd entered a different time dimension. With no light it's like we're cave dwellers again, trying desperately to retain a connection to our own time, to law and order, to ourselves, the song safeguarding the weak thread so it doesn't break.

But that was childhood of course, and though there were electric lights, oil lamps hadn't yet been completely supplanted. But neither of them were used as much as now. Remember to turn off the light. Did you turn it off? There weren't as many switches either—just one in each room —seconds of darkness as you moved through the house between turning lights off at one location until you reached safety at the next switch.

Today we protect ourselves against darkness as if it were a disease, like against contagion by a disease that is so eradicated that no one catches it anymore or knows what it is. Anywhere near a city at night a cloud of light floats overhead. Copenhagen lights up half of Sjælland. Plus there are streetlights, house lights, headlights from vehicles everywhere. The dark is pushed back. The basic condition for half our lifetimes once has now become unapproachable, treacherous, dangerous darkness. The dark like it was, when you couldn't get around it, was threatening, dreaded. And now, it's like something else is lost along with the loss of darkness—a reality—yet it is still there. It willingly appears—just a little crack and it's there, in all its original glory, undiminished as if it had never been gone.

We remember the war as dark times, also literally, although the technical blackout was only outside. Indoors we existed in pools of light similar to conditions long ago.

How did people in times past remember the winter? As dark times. Black times. Darkness has spread itself like a heaviness in our souls as in our language, so that "dark" times are not meant only literally. And the poor lighting methods they had at their disposal were only used when it was necessary for work or another situation where they had to be able to see.

I spent one fall on a farm in Norway and one evening the mistress sent me on an errand to the neighbor's farm. "What if they're in bed? I asked. "You can just wake them up," she told me. From a distance I could already see that they must have gone to bed—there were no lights on anywhere. I had a flashlight to help me at the rough places on the path. I used it, too, when I knocked on their door, and when I came into the entry and began to knock on more doors. "Come in," someone said. I opened the door and stood there looking into a completely dark room. I'd turned off the flashlight. You don't just shine lights into strange people's living rooms. I explained where I came from and told them my errand. "Yes, sure, I think we can take care of that," said a voice in the dark. "Oh, you're a Dane and you're living there, well, all right," and we chatted a bit. But then I did need to borrow that one thing. I hear the man get up from his chair and after a moment I hear the clink of a lamp glass and a match is struck, and the light from the lamp fights its way outward. Spread around in the room, eight or nine people are sitting there—old, young—a whole family plus farmhands.

That's the way people gathered. With a grounding in darkness. They were their own entertainment, had television inside themselves.

People were familiar with darkness in the olden days. We can imagine how it was. Like a lightning bug it rummages in our consciousness, a decidedly antiquated situation, something that was left behind on the surface from antediluvian layers of tales and reports, something that has made an extra impression, because it was fundamental like a family memory. The situation occurred repeatedly. A person went out at night and lost their way, then caught a glimpse of a light far off in the distance and walked towards it: a house, a residence, a candle flame behind a window. The person walked towards the light as if it were a star.

In this way Blicher must have walked across his Jylland heaths at night. "I stopped at times to ascertain if the light had moved. No!—therefore it could not be a lantern or a watchman; but must be one of those secretive meteors, that are believed to signify buried treasure or buried corpses. Of the former I was not afraid, even less of the latter; I kept going. The glare steadily increased in size and clarity."

Darkness was something that used to be present; it was a daily occurrence; it was the way things were.

Fourteen hours darkness. Sixteen hours darkness. Half of life they lived in darkness. So much so they must have felt that that was the basic element.

The calendar year itself ended for them like a light going out, like the light went out for me, just the embers on the wick of the last small candle after the splendors of summer. There they sat remembering the dying vision of a light like a memory on the retina, while they fumbled their way through the tunnel to the new year.

You sit with a candle, by a clear burning flame and have a blind date with the darkness.

The darkness—this substance there hardly are words for, but just is there; this absence which is so difficult to describe clearly, because all the descriptions begin with this basic element of darkness; this condition against which you could toss all diminutives, all verbal abuse, if you didn't feel at the same time that it were in vain, because it is the essential, the original, the wordless silence itself—and that all degrees of light, ourselves, and everything we know that needs words are like a rash, just a passing illness from lack of darkness.

The Glint of Blue

If I happened to be abroad and felt homesick for Denmark, it would not surprise me if it were the water—the waters —that I longed for. Certainly, if it were not particular regions or cities that I was thinking about. If the longing were simply discomfort at being where I was and the awareness of something better left behind, if it were not longing for certain people or places, were not concrete thoughts but just an abstract longing. If someone observed my downheartedness and said, *What is it you are pining for?*, then I know, that before I made it from the abstract to the concrete, before I had time to think, in my inner eye I would see a glint of blue—water.

The water, the Danish navigable waters, are the country's most characteristic feature. Every time I have traveled—enough at any rate, that it was unavoidable to get to know new parts of the country, acquire some new experience—there have appeared sudden glints of blue: I crossed water.

Bridges—the Great Stream Bridge and the Little Belt Bridge. There is a different sound and feel when you travel on them. The sound of the car motor and the rattling of the train cars change tone when suddenly blended with air and wind. Your own relationship to the train changes. What is most important is no longer the compartment in the particular car in which you are riding. Your perception expands. You become suddenly aware of the whole line of train cars. The long line of cars coupled behind a locomotive feels intense, as the remarkable traveling entity it is. You are being lifted from province to province, ships like toys deep below, seemingly motionless, fixed like compass needles but with their bows declaring the direction of their desires.

Of course I have often been down there myself traveling on that level.

Masned Sound—the Great Stream. One whole summer I crossed it every Saturday night and every Monday morning, driven by love.

Isn't it often infatuations that we can thank for particular knowledge of a vicinity, whether urban or rural? Otherwise I have never had any business on the islands of Lolland-Falster. I remember from my trips southward the bright Saturday evenings on my motorcycle. Not because I saw so much—it was only a five horsepower romance making headway. Would I make the ferry? And when I finally arrived at the hills before land's end at Vordingborg, the sound lay spread before my eyes. The glint of blue. I'd made it. And when in the Monday dawn I neared the water again at the tiny fishing village of Orehoved, I felt the salt-water air in my nostrils and accordingly re-entered the gray everyday by driving aboard the ferry's wet planks.

Then there is the Little Belt crossing. By me personally this channel has always been crossed at night. From my childhood I remember the air of panic in the darkness and lamplight. That channel was so narrow. There was no repose like at the Great Belt. It was like just having to switch trains. Already long before arriving to it, you stood in line in the train vestibule—the idea was to get on board early. Nervous adults grabbed you by the hand as soon as the train stopped. Running along you were borne over the platform with the luggage. What mattered was getting down quickly to the ferry, to get a good seat, to stand at the front of the line where disembarking would occur. We wanted to be at the front of the crab-like chasséing advance through the train aisles, past compartment after compartment to find one that was empty, completely empty, where we could toss our luggage into the rack, triumphantly settle in and take a breather from the stress while crabs, with luggage and children in their claws, hurried sideways down the aisle. And our own compartment, which we once had to ourselves, became packed, shared with new arrivals with fresh stress in their eyes. Little Belt—the channel itself—on those trips it was perceived only as a flash of black water, as a sucking sound against a wharf.

No, I don't think I ever rode that ferry during the day, but this must just be coincidence. Though once I did miss it. It was when I was on a bike trip with a friend; and we didn't wait for the next one. A private ferryman was tacking in the harbor in a sailboat, cruising in the blue water with Jylland in the background. He took us and our bicycles on board and sailed us across. We sat straddling the thwarts in shorts, close to the sun-reflecting waves clucking and smacking against the little boat. The fare was the same.

Now those waters are deserted. The Little Belt Bridge has covered over the memories, has appeared like a colossal silver fin across the landscape, towering between the hills, visible from many miles away.

One day a Great Belt Bridge might appear like that too, a shining highway of steel and concrete disappearing into the blue, a divider between past and present, a line erasing and changing something essential in our Danish daily life.

What a role the passages over the Great Belt have played for us—they have been an indispensable part of our lives. A cup of coffee and a piece of coffee cake together with a stuffed seagull should be on display at the National Museum. We would nod wistfully to the display case, nod to something essential in our past. Yes, this is how it was to be a Dane in the old days.

As on a flickering screen we would see our life's passages between Sjælland and Fyn.

I have sailed there on bitter winter days, on crossings that took many hours. The ferry could only move forward a few yards at a time and otherwise held still, waiting in the midst of all that white under a heavy gray sky, while the icebreaker in front made its approaches forward and back, smashing a narrow channel through the ice. I have sailed there on sparkling Easter holidays when waves and seagulls seemed new—new and fresh like the air I sucked in, like the season just beginning. And I have sailed there on great consummate summer days, when the seagulls' cries didn't seem so agitated any more and their soaring flight didn't seem as nervous or watchful. The water was different, too. When I stared down at it over the side, the water evoked a deep complete rest, relaxed—a world of its own whose depths my vision could enter, along with thousands of huge red jellyfish as anchoring points of perspective.

The journey over the Great Belt—a pattern, a melody, a theme with variations—experiences so familiar they are like language itself: gulls catching scraps of bread in the air; that one passenger every time who stands with arms slanting upwards, determined that the birds eat from his hand; the crumpled lunch refuse on the tables; the empty shoebox tossed overboard now floating on the water, left behind and growing smaller and smaller and more and more solitary while little children hang over the railing, following it entranced with their eyes; the smell of coffee and the sound of bottles in the restaurant. The Great Belt Ferry: the ship where everyone feels at home; the restaurant that has a whole population as regulars. Well, not everyone. Because also in this picture belong those who remain sitting down in the recesses of the ferry—the strange ones, that particular species which does not move from their berths in the train. When I rose up liberated for a change of scenery and fresh air I didn't notice that they stayed in place. I realized this first when I returned to the compartment again, in the way they looked at me. It's the same way livestock in a stable turn their gaze towards someone approaching from the outside world. The air in the berth reveals this, too. Some people travel like that. Elderly women take a seat and stay sitting, remain like that in their hats and coats, hands resting on their bags and packages on their laps from Copenhagen to Lemvig, eating their egg sandwiches in secret, when everyone else has left the compartment.

One cannot travel in Denmark more than a few hours before being interrupted by a glint of blue. One particular summer vacation is perhaps a bad example. You can't go by the fact that we rode the ferry from Hundested to Grenå; it was just that we had had enough of Sjælland. And when, in addition to that, we routed our bike tour around the perimeter of the Limfjord, you can't go by all the blue we saw there either. But still! Our trip led from bridge to ferry, from ferry to bridge. Those were our goals out ahead: different fjords, sounds and channels: Fegge Sound, Agger Sound, Vil Sound, Salling Sound, plus another crossing between Salling and Mors. We raised a flag in the air according to instructions on the beach. When the ferry man on the other side saw it, he came sailing in his boat with a barge to carry the bicycles. For half an hour we stood there on the beach, hearing and watching his approach. Half an hour while a ferry arrived from the past.

How many different ferry stations are there in Denmark? How many places must the traveler commit himself to the waves in order to proceed? I remember a particular day trip, when I drove a couple of hundred miles by car, yet still the day consisted mostly of boat trips, water and more water, driving on and off of ferries, successive ticket offices and successive ticket collectors, wharves where people stood watching while I sailed away, and wharves where people stood there watching while I disembarked. There were new promenade decks that I walked up on, new vistas over the water, and water, seagulls and new seagulls. Korsør-Lohals, Rudkøbing-Vemmenæs, Vindeby-Svendborg.... The weather was good that day, so in my memory it all appears as a flickering of blue water and twinkling sunshine, bicycles with heavy packs, bare legs and sandals springing up and down stairways, people at railings with their heads back and faces turned towards the wind from the sea.

But of course I also remember passages under different conditions. The deep throbbing cabins I have sat protected in when the weather was bad. People looked different then, quieter, sunken into themselves. Their movements were different, slower; their faces different—quieter and more rigid. Even if the ferry weren't rocking, still it was as if we were under the influence of the changed weather, like we were in a trance, quiet inside ourselves. We were just traveling and therefore placed here, listening to the throbbing motor. We looked at the King and Queen behind framed glass, stole a few glances at our fellow passengers, but averted our eyes if they looked back. Even children were different— silent and out-of-sorts. Only infants and drunken men were unaffected and uncomprehending. Babies had bright-red faces from crying and screaming—there is hardly room inside them for that howl—they are about to explode! There is hardly room in the compartment for it, and still it seemed far away, far from a great stillness that looks at them with eyes as if from behind a glass and frame.

But maybe it is because they comprehend something, that babies so often cry in lower berths. And perhaps the same is true of the gathering at the table with the numerous green bottles, standing and rattling against one another. Their boisterousness contrasts completely with the mood around them. Does it also feel to them like it's just an act they are putting on, forcing—a spiteful gallows clamor? The participants come and go when those kind of gatherings have lasted long enough—they are never all present at once. They drink with ghost partners, take turns disappearing to the rest room. Best of luck to them. I know what ferry toilets can be like in bad weather.

The hiss of the wind when you leave your berth and push open the door to the outside—the roar of the waves. The pelting rain and the wet greasy deck. Shivering, pale people, huddled in corners, who were seeking shelter and fresh air at the same time. And maybe some calves who were tied together in a corner with heads lowered. If the ferry were rocking they stood with splayed legs, and if it were pitching heavily, they would alternate sprawling and skating around in their own slippery droppings, trying to stand up again. The animals should not be forgotten—livestock on their first and last journey. They belong to the daily routine of the ferry crossing.

It is relatively rare that I have ridden the ferry and the animals have made an impression on me. Mostly it happens when I stand at a dock and watch the ferry arriving. Here comes the ferry. And I saunter down and I take my place on the dock with my hands in my pockets along with the others who are watching the ferry arrive, all reverently present at the familiar traffic ritual. The clanging from the bridge, the shower from the screw when it is put in reverse, the ferry's thud against the dock planks, the mooring line tossed to shore. And out swarm pedestrians and bicyclists, scooters and cars, groups with people to greet them and happy reunions; also small cheery familiar rituals. I could have prompted them, but it is unnecessary—the performance has taken place thousands of times. And afterwards, the clean-up behind the scenery when the audience has left—beer bottles, bottled gas, and the livestock. The butcher, with his apron the color of the Danish flag, has come to receive them: the shrieking pigs, the silent reluctant calves. I myself am a silent bystander. I can stand and watch animals like that for a long time, how they are pulled and pushed—animals that otherwise are not obstinate, but now are afraid. Sometimes they have to be hit with canes. It can be done more or less brutally. I remember a man from Fyn who twisted the animals' tails and smacked them on their rumps, but maybe didn't do it so hard. He did it with a different attitude. Apparently to calm himself—and them—he kept repeating in his soft sing-song dialect: "Don't worry! It'll all work out! You'll see!"

Someday when all ferries are abolished, when you can without hindrance drive from the one end of the country to the other—of course it will be practical—something will be missing.

There is a story about a man from India who had flown to a conference in Europe. The first few days he would not leave his hotel room. And when he was asked why he didn't take part in the meetings he answered: "My soul has not arrived yet!"

Maybe this is the secret is of our Danish ferries, the reason I delight in them. Thanks to their interruptions my soul has a chance to catch up, so it can follow along with me as I travel from province to province.

*   *   *   *

Translator's note: The Great Belt Bridge between Sjælland and Fyn, the third largest suspension bridge in the world, was completed in 1997, eliminating the Great Belt Ferry.

The Hawthorns

I dropped my bike at the roadside and walked across the field to a particular tree trunk I know that you can sit on. My shoes took on a grayish hue from the road dust, and I carefully wiped them off on the grass. After I sat down in the shade I noticed how hot I had become; it was just after noon and the sun was high in the sky. There were no deer in sight, but all around various artists were browsing. They were busy, because the hawthorns were in full bloom. Three of the artists were ladies standing in a row a couple of yards apart. Clearly watercolor. From a seaside boarding house. I counted twelve artists in all, and I wondered if I would end up in one of the paintings if I sat perfectly still.

Around the tree, lungwort grew with its small blue and purple flowers, and the plants hung their heads wearily in the noonday heat. At the base the trunk was half hollow and so punky that a stinging nettle plant had taken root there. A little viridian beetle came trotting up my pants leg. It started at the cuff, stopped a couple of times to assess the situation, but continued anyway, fresh and eager to go all the way up. I have seen small children like this, who of their own accord and full of purpose, suddenly run ten steps away from their mother, stand still a second—where you can see that the world, so great and new, already has absorbed them—and then run ten more steps into the adventure, before being caught up by their mother's arm.

Then suddenly there are a few seconds of complete silence. Evidently an endless chain of cars had been noisily motoring by on the road outside Deer Park without my taking notice until now, when the chain was broken. I listen, perk up my ears as if panicked by the quiet that suddenly envelops me. Has the world been deserted by sound? But then the air above me begins to intone a golden quivering, sort of like how one might imagine the bowing of a violin would sound after the strings are loosened. Is it summertime itself making that sound? I look up and, in the hawthorn's crown over my head, bees are flying from one white flower cluster to the next, affectionately violating flower after flower, and the intoxicating aroma descends on me together with the sound, enclosing me in a dome of sweet, complete summer-ness.

Thin, white clouds which have no influence on the weather are making their way across the blue sky. Swallows race by, adding their chirps in flight as tones in the orchestra. Far away a cuckoo clucks, so far away that the sound seems blurred, disappearing in distant treetops. Chaffinches start sounding off, and into the whole thing suddenly a nightingale chimes in. A nightingale, in the middle of the day, in shimmering sunshine! I have heard them before, and it is as if one is not listening a nightingale to at all. It feels like an exaggeration, almost an embarrassment. The mood grows hysterical. The season in its culmination is going off the rails, like a clock whose regulator has failed so the spring races audibly through the works, dragging after it tolls on the hour and the half hour, so they trip on one another's heels.

Then from a little pond, on the other side of the dusty road, an underground reprimand is uttered: "Hey there, just a second. May a frog at this unconventional moment have permission to raise his voice and make one small remark. Just a reminder that there are others around, and that we also have the right to be present. I have nothing else to say, but some people think they own everything." This croaking was delivered like a sober protest, a subterranean wisdom, just barely hinting at a secret that no power could force it to reveal. But then just wait until tonight!

I have sat on that hawthorn trunk in the evening, listening to the frogs. First a croak from one side of the pond. And then an answer from the other side. Then again from the first side, and then from the other side, and then one from a distinctly third place. More and more chime in, deep and high croaks overlapping, a rhythmic unfolding and a rhythmic crescendo, reminding me of African drumming. And then always after this a quite jungle-like stillness. I have tried sneaking over to the pond when the concert was at its peak, but silence always came suddenly before I reached it. I have tried standing quiet as a mouse, letting the mosquitoes bite me, figuring that in the end the frogs would forget I was there or would start to think I was a tree. But not a sound; just the mirrored surface. A single time a twig floated on the water, but I knew it was a frog, since I had just seen it swim a couple of strokes. And its eyes were still visible—the shiny black eyeballs twinkling up at me. If I really thought I could pretend I was a tree, then it could just as well pretend it was a twig at the same time. And when eventually I began to have doubts—Was it a twig after all?—and I tossed in a clump of dirt, it casually dove down as if to say, "Okay, there we learned something about both of us, didn't we?" And then it wasn't even there to look at any more.

I walked over to the water again that afternoon. Small white flowers—frogbit or arrowhead—flowed like a carpet all along the bank, and on the other side there was a starling bathing and two painters painting. They wanted that serene pond for the foreground and then behind it the savannah-like field with the scattered hawthorns. In the afternoon's sharp light the flowering hawthorn crowns took on the appearance of cloth, like heavy brocade with interwoven silver. And then perhaps a tall oak near the edge, because its leaves were a paler green than the hawthorns.

Where the road from Rødeport to Rødebro passes by Springforbi the hawthorns are spread across a large part of the Hermitage field. They are like scattered tree islands, so ancient and distinctive that foreign foresters make visits to view them. Several hundred years old, and most of them deformed by deers' nibbling, the thick trunks twist hither and thither over the earth. The trees resemble torture petrified, or a stylized death struggle. A couple of them look as if they had been struck by terror and panic as soon as they raised their heads in this vale of tears. Their trunks undulate horizontally over the ground as if they are looking for a hole in which to disappear down into again as quickly as possible.

But still they have grown to be several hundred years old, and when June arrives, they flower.

By the way, the best time to see them is not early in the afternoon, but late in the evening, when the white canopies are at rest in the moonlight and the stillness. This is when one can emerge from the darkness of the road between the tall beeches onto the field under the open summer night sky, and the hawthorns stand as islands bathed in moonlight. Then it is like looking into a dreamworld of beauty and harmony.

My mother knew this. Through the years she took me there evenings when the hawthorns were in blossom. It wasn't because we had any particular attachment to the place, since we were from a totally different part of the country. It was only after my father's death that we moved to Sjælland. It was just to—well, just to see them. I was a little boy and I remember that we drove a long way with the trolley and then afterwards walked far, late in the evening, through the dark woods. It was a rather odd thing to do, and the only reason that I didn't protest was because I knew that we would go to Bellevue Beach afterwards and I would get a dish of ice cream. Finally we would arrive to the field and nothing would happen, except there, out on the edge, still with the tall trees from the road shadowing us, the old lady would stand still for a moment and look out at the hawthorns in the moonlight; stand there just for a moment, just a few seconds, silently, shaking her head just slightly, as if at something she saw or something she thought. And then she would turn around. And then I would know that at last we could start the journey homeward.

Good heavens, she was only thirty-five at the time.

Perhaps she was weeping, deep down inside.

And that she never went any closer! After all, we had ridden for half an hour on the trolley and walked for forty-five minutes. And we could see—we *saw* that just a couple of hundred steps ahead it would be really beautiful, in all its glory!

She would just stand there looking, as if she had lost herself in it, and then turn back.

Of course there were also years when we didn't make it out there. Times when the season had passed and she could see that we missed it this year. When she thought this for a moment, she would look up from her work, stare absently, lost, shaking her head slightly as if to show that it didn't matter anyway. Then she would bend over her work again. And one particular year, the last, when by then I was a young man, I wasn't taken along for the trip. Instead, begrudgingly, I took her. But even then we didn't come any closer than there where the field began. Even then we stood just where the dark road ended, partly because it was always there that we turned back, and partly because I had a secret agenda of cutting the trip short, since I knew there was a girl in a red jacket that I could meet on Deer Park Hill.

I remember then that she took a few steps away from the road towards one solitary hawthorn and smelled one of the white flower clusters. She reached for it, brought it down to her level, and there was something young and almost thankful in her movement. I had allowed her time for that.

And that's how it goes!

But if I were to "come back" then I know it's there I would meet her. But not standing like a stranger on the edge. We would be far in, at home among the moonlit hawthorns.

A Ride with a Lady

It was one of those periods when the sun and oppressive heat suddenly emerged after a month of wind and cold. I went riding in eastern Jylland with a young lady who knew the area. From an open field we could see Skamlingsbanken to the south. She pointed it out as the tallest of three hills of nearly equal height, and when we squinted we could just see the obelisk like a nail on the peak. She rode with imagination, turning off at small farm roads where the horses could gallop in the soft wheel ruts. She pushed her way into the woods through holes in the bushes that she knew from previous rides. The horses forced the branches aside with their heads to make way, and we had to duck low against their hot sweaty necks not to get hit when the branches swung back. We trotted through young pine tree plantings, where the brown grass reached the horses' chests, and where willowherbs stood with their red stems like lights at a harbor fest. We rode down hills and up hills, in tandem over small stony creeks down in the ravines, in laborious climbs up slopes, except when she preferred to gallop straight up, so the horses' back legs tensed as if in spasm. At one place there was a wide gully with a bridge, but no, she knew the bridge was rotted and we would risk a hoof going through and the horse breaking its leg. So she turned in between the trees, then turned directly toward the gully. The black Holsteiner gathered itself and stretched beneath her, snorting with excitement. A snap of the whip as a farewell to this side, and it flew and landed with forelegs and rear legs and all its weight in the new world. It sped in between the young trees cracking the branches, kicked its back legs skyward in sheer excitement, was ready to gallop to the end of the world. But she got him turned around and calmed down, and there we were on either side of the gully. And she was waiting for me.

Until then I was enthusiastic. The ride had been ten times better with her along, since we could talk and yell to one another, and because she knew all the good places to ride in this area. Otherwise I would have just ridden straight up the road and back again. But now a damper had been put on my excitement. If I had been alone I would never have made it to this gully. If I had been riding with a man, I could have said, "No, thank you very much. You won't find me risking life and limb hazarding a two- to three-yard chasm." But I was not alone, and I was with a young girl.

"That was very nice," I said with appreciation, as if I had only held my horse back so I could judge her performance. Then I backed up my horse, gave it an approach as if it were going to jump from the island of Langeland to Tåsinge. Using both spurs and whip, my whole life breathlessly passing before my eyes, remembering particularly my childhood piousness, I stormed toward the gully, which gaped like an open mass grave. Are we jumping or are we not jumping? Is the horse coming or am I going over alone? But the horse chose to come along, hurtling forward like a tank. It took flight as if by an explosion, and the twigs on the other side whipped me in my ears. Then we stopped and she, for whom I had risked my limbs, patted the horse and laughed.

She was ten years old. While trotting, the horse lifted her so high in the air that I could see blue sky between her and the saddle. But she was totally comfortable, landing securely on the horse's back after each flight.

We emerged between green meadows and yellow fields of grain. Oh grain! Oh sugar beets! Oh potatoes! I thought dutifully to myself. Oh bounty of the earth! But this local lady also in this context brought me far from the city dweller's beaten trail. It was Petersen's oats. They looked very nice. On the other hand, the barley farther away didn't look so good. "Why not?" I asked.

"When the barley is ripe, you shouldn't be able to see the tracks of the sowing machine," she said, and looked at me puzzled.

No, of course not.

And all that straw this year. On one of her father's fields the grain was this far over her head. She showed me how far. In the loft of their barn they had a stone marten. What did it look like? It looked like they always look. Hadn't she seen it? No, she had never seen it. One of her teachers at school was so dumb. Once she had done something to so and so, and then he had said so and so, but it wasn't her fault, now was it? No, of course not. Boy, was he dumb; but then everyone thinks so. And he was so ugly too, and then he still acted so full of himself.

Then she started galloping again. Like the perfect hostess she had a surprise for me: obstacles set up on a narrow forest path and a couple of them quite high. I folded my fingers around the reins, closed my eyes and followed after her. Once I was lying on the ground while the horse, big as an elephant, walked around and over me with all its legs near my face. I got up on it again without her noticing the mishap.

"I'll bet you couldn't have found those obstacles on your own," she said when we were together again. I admitted she was right.

We resumed trotting, and now suddenly a gentle air of sorrow and tragedy took over her mood. Just look at the tail on her horse, how thin it was. Once, out in the fields, someone had cut it all off because horsehair had gotten so expensive. In the morning the horse stood there and didn't have anything to swat away the flies with and looked so miserable, as if it knew how ugly it had become. Another time a horse in the barn stepped on her kitten and killed it, a white one, and the kitten's mother had eaten some of her prettiest pigeons. And another horse stepped in some barbed wire by accident and got an infection in its leg. And the first time it was supposed to be shoed and the blacksmith touched that leg, it took off from the stall and jumped headfirst right into the brick wall so it died on the spot. But they could have been more careful—her father and the blacksmith and all of them. If it had been they who had a bad leg then they would have been careful....

We had arrived at the fjord and rode the horses right out into the water's edge. They splashed with pleasure in the low water and the coolness rose up toward us.

"Let's take the saddles off, then ride all the way out and let them swim," she said excitedly.

"I'm not so sure about that," I said.

"We have to. It's so good for them."

Still, I distanced myself from the idea. I felt that now my life depended on being steadfast. But it was no use. After we had our bathing suits on, we rode out. The water rose to the horses' bellies, to their chests. Only with persuasion and struggle were we able to keep them moving forward. Suddenly the bottom disappeared under them. In a glimpse I saw her face turned toward mine with an expression that was supposed to show all our mutual enjoyment. The horses were thrashing around, fighting to keep their frightened heads above water and get back to land. In one moment's panic they tried climbing up on one another to have something to walk on. She just laughed.

Afterward we agreed to take it easy. For the horses' sake. A great relief from heaven and the fjord came over me when we then turned homeward. Politely she began to discuss art and literature. She liked movies better than theater. More happens in movies.

"Like for example in *Gøngehøvdingen*," I said. Yes, she would agree. Like *Gøngehøvdingen*. Then again, maybe she liked the theater better after all. It was just that in movies you can see them coming and going. For example, if someone is attacked, or a girl gets lost on her way home, you can see it in the film. In the theater they just stand there yapping about it telling what happened. But when something finally does happen in the theater, she thinks that they do it better.

She had dropped her reins and leaned an elbow against the horse's neck, while she spoke reasonably. It was like she lived on that horse.

"I really like slow hymns," she said. "They give you such good thoughts." She laughed embarrassedly and sat up straight. I nodded solemnly and didn't so much as blink. We were nearing sacred territory now. I had won her confidence. And she talked about the moral difficulties that adults caused her. They were often so strange. When visitors came, they could say, "Really! That was funny! How nice! That was so sweet of you!" And then when the visitors left they would say, "Boy, are they boring. I could hardly stand it."

She turned her snub nose toward me. There was anguish in her eyes.

"Isn't that strange? Can't they just not say things like that? And maybe the others thought that *they* were boring. What makes them think that they themselves are so funny and pleasant?"

She rode in front down the path, which I would never have found either, and when we came out, we stopped on a spot with the most gorgeous view over the fjord and the channel. She looked proud and expectant on my behalf. The highlight of the ride.

"Wouldn't you rather have ridden with someone else?" she asked.

"With someone else?" I said.

"Yeah, with one of the grown-ups," she said, without looking at me.
"Not at all. I like riding with you better than anybody."
"Oh, that's not true. And I know it," she said, satisfied.

     *   *   *   *

Translator's Note: Gøngehøvdingen is the tale of Sven Poulsen Gønge, captain of the Danish freedom fighters against Sweden in the 1660s. His life was portrayed in books and film, and more recently, in theater and television.

Safari on Mors Island

During the period immediately following the war, when it was still difficult to get car tires, I was on a road trip in Jylland with a friend. The car was from 1933 and, apparently, so were the tires. On the 50 km drive from Ringkøbing to Skive we had seven flats. We made a tour out of it. If we drove over fifteen miles an hour the tires would go flat - except the spare - all at once, due to the enormous heat generated in the rubber by the friction on the road surface. The spare tire went flat independently of this. It hung on the back of the car and went flat either because of too much sun, or too much rain, or possibly because sharp pebbles were being kicked up at it. Once we had it vulcanized at an auto shop in a small town. The vulcanizer pumped it up and rolled it out from the shop to the front yard and through the gate to our car. As it passed through the gate it went flat.

But we had a good time nevertheless. We saw the landscape in a relaxed tempo and with plenty of stops. In the evening we sought out hilltops, preferably in rather unpopulated areas, where we could spend the night. We would leave the car there and walk, each with suitcase in hand, to an inn or hotel. The advantage was that the next morning we would not have to be towed by a Falck tow truck or a local mechanic, like we had done several times. The difficulties starting, which the motor invariably experienced in the cool morning hours, were more easily overcome when the start was downhill.

We eventually arrived in Skive, and a few days later made it all the way up to Mors. It is gorgeous there: Legind Mountain, Salge Hill, Man-Rock. We photographed ourselves up on Legind Mountain's forest-covered slopes with the Limfjord in the background. First he posed out on the edge of a cliff while I climbed up in a tree in order to take the picture of him, so that both some young birch trees behind him and the fjord below would be in it. I wanted him to move over, to get him placed better in the picture, but that would have resulted in his falling seventy feet down the cliff. So instead I laid down halfway out on a dangerously spindly branch. Then it was my turn out on the cliff, and he climbed up into the tree.

"Are you ready?" he yelled to warn me.

"Yes," I replied, keeping the caramel candy still in my mouth while turning my best profile towards him. Then I heard the branch crack and his falling through the tree. But he got the picture. I still have both of them. We are each standing with our jackets flapping in the wind, looking solitarily outward, gripped by the spectacular vista. Ships are sailing on the Limfjord down below and in the distance.

We had decided to travel cheaply. The numerous repair bills for the tires made this difficult, but we did our best. Dry inns. Daily specials. And we furnished our own lunches. Stuffed into biscuit tins we had delicacies packed in waxed paper. In good weather we threw ourselves down by the roadside and feasted, while we listened to the bees and the birds. When it rained we ate in the car, drops thrumming on the windows, but this was more difficult. Once we spilled a jar of pickled herring on the backseat, and after that we always had to drive with a couple of the windows down. One day, when it had rained all morning, but then suddenly cleared up with blue sky and sunshine over the dripping wet fields, we set our lunch spread right in the middle of the road. That was my idea. We had turned off the main road onto a narrow asphalt side road which looked as if no one ever drove on it. We parked the car to one side, began unpacking and opening jars, and arranged the lunch across the roadway by the running board, where we sat. It took a while, but also came to look festive and inviting. Much more hygienic and with better access than when you sit on a field or a road edge, where different items are constantly hiding themselves between clumps of grass and getting spilled and having creatures crawling on them when you finally find them. If, for example, you wanted some garfish in oil, it was just four steps to the other side of the road. There you go, garfish in oil! Then you could put it on your bread and either stand up eating it or set back down on the running board with it, whatever your pleasure. And there we sat with sunshine in our faces and with swallows crossing low between our beer bottles and over the waxed paper with the liver paté. We had small jars with numerous little delicacies, triangles of cream cheese, bags with tomatoes, slices of bread, packets of butter, and whatever else the heart desires. Lovely. Life was great. A cow was standing in the field.

"Hey, you know this was my idea," I said.

Out on the main road a bus approached, and the driver shouted and waved enthusiastically to us. "Thanks!" we yelled and waved back. What else could anyone say to us but Bon appetit! or God bless! We raised our bottles, drank and toasted the driver and his passengers. Then we took our knives and reached for the bread. Now we were really going to dig in.

A couple of seconds later the bus turned onto our side road, and with brakes squealing, stopped with a tremendous steaming radiator just in front of our culinary roadblock. This was its route. This was its asphalt we had set our table on. The driver and a half score interested passengers hung out the windows, while we, bent over, raced around on the road, packing our things together to make way. With the last items in our arms we watched the bus pass and disappear. When it was gone, we caught sight of a horse and buggy slowly advancing from the opposite direction, and we realized that it wasn't worth laying it all out again. Hunger gnawed at us. We fantasized about a bench somewhere. Someplace along the road there had to be a bench to sit on. And we were going to find that bench. My friend sat behind the wheel and I stayed outside to keep an eye on our lunch on the running board. A procession across Mors. Beer in hand, I trod the wet sun-reflecting country road beside this solemn, onward-rolling buffet.

Late in the afternoon we reached Mors Island's northernmost point, the long table-topped isthmus—Feggeklit—with its ferry transport across Fegge Sound to Thy on the other side. I was irritated. Earlier my friend had asked me to tour a mo-clay factory in the company of its chief engineer. I hate that kind of thing more than anything, but since we were nearby the country's only mo-clay plant, he thought that we ought to see it. So we were ushered around a factory area in a confusion of stone and ovens and conveyor belts, while he asked questions and acted as if he understood what the engineer explained to us. I also had to be polite and act interested. As the tour progressed, I came to understand less and less about mo-clay. It still makes me depressed just thinking about it. There were no living creatures in the factory but the three of us, but all around us was chopping and whirring, rattling and throwing up of dust. Our feet got wet, our hats got white and we got silt in our mouths. A conveyor belt rolled out piles of clay that kneaded themselves, cut themselves into pieces, rode into ovens and came out of ovens and cooled down and packed themselves and stacked themselves up. If I had sat down on one of those conveyor belts, in two hours I would have been sailed away to the ends of the earth as uniform parcels of sound-insulating material that displayed both the Danish flag and Danish ingenuity.

At the foot of Feggeklit I made him stop the car.

"Hamlet's father," I said, and pointed up the cliff.

"Why in the world should we care about Hamlet's father?" he said, confused.

"Since we're here, we have to see it," I said, and began shuffling my way up the steep hillside, while he sat in the car scowling.

"How can we stop one mile from the ferry dock?" he shouted to me suddenly. "There might be a ferry sitting there we could get on. We should have been in Skagen four days ago!"

At the top of the cliff there was a stone with something on it about Hamlet's father or grandfather. But the view was impressive and made the ascent worthwhile. I could see across the Limfjord to Thisted and almost to the city of Ålborg.

When we reached the ferry dock, it turned out he was right. The ferry had just left. We could see it out in the current, disappearing towards Thy on the opposite shore.

The next ferry wouldn't be for another three hours. So we sat inside the cozy ferry restaurant and had some eel. Afterwards we dallied along the beach before returning to the restaurant where other cars had arrived and guests were seated at the tables in the dining room. My friend, who had gone off on his own before the restaurant entry, came in at another door, so it appeared as if he had entered from one of the inner rooms. Suddenly he stood in the doorway, then greeted people at every single table with small bows and smiles, rubbed his hands and said hello and bon appetit, which, of course there is no law against.

And they loved it and insisted on greeting him and sharing a glass with him. And when they said it was a really nice place, he said that he liked it too. And when they said that the food was excellent, he said that he knew they were doing their best out in the kitchen. His motto had always been: Anything for the customers. Whether the profit was a bit more or a bit less, truth be told, had never interested him. With that, he was offered both beers and bitters.

Now I really don't like that kind of thing. I hate when someone takes a joke so far that it becomes dishonest. Those people were being charitable and were deceived. Instead, he could have, with a little wave, motioned to me and said that I was his brother or brother-in-law, who was like his right hand and that none of this would have come to fruition if it hadn't been for me. Then I might have been able to go along with it; but he didn't think of that.

Fegge Sound is, by the way, a picturesque place. The narrow isthmus with its high cliffs pokes its way from south to north into the Limfjord. Standing on the tip, it's as if you are standing on an island with water all around you. I discovered later too, that regardless of which Limfjord coast you happen to be on, you can always see Feggeklit appearing like a distant mountain range out of the water. The restaurant, as I said, was cozy, with nationally-famous pan-roasted eel. The ferry is infrequent, very likely privately-owned by the restauranteur. In any case it's he who captains it, a formidable steel ship with smokestack and bridge. From a distance it resembles an Atlantic Ocean steamship. It just has the peculiarity that as it approaches, it doesn't get any larger. Completely opposite of most ships, it gets smaller and smaller, while you yourself stand at the dock growing to supernatural size.

Two Jylland horses, which were going the same way as us, made the ferry sway considerably when they were pulled on board. After them came a small flatbed truck loaded with two pigs and cages with hens, besides three men, two women and a couple of children of the same breed as the horses, and finally, our car. When it was all in place, the headlights and bumper stuck out over the hatchway on the one side of the ferry, while the trunk and half of the rear wheels floated over the waves on the other side. During the trip any passage to or from the stern had to occur through our car. The captain and ticket boy, men and women, everyone had to squeeze themselves across the carseats, in one door and out the other. We felt like amusement park attendants, when the flood of people is about to get out of control at the turnstiles. But we were glad that the horses didn't seem to need to move.

During the crossing it got darker and darker, and more and more whitecaps appeared on the waves. Low clouds and a high sea came driving in from the west. When we neared the long low cement pier on the Thy side, night was falling and waves washed over the pier's farthest point. The farmers grabbed the horses' bridles and we got into our car. Everyone was in a hurry to get onto land and away. We had places to go. When the ferry was moored, we started the car and the captain went to open up for us.

That is when the obvious happened. The car had gotten a flat while parked on the ferry. The one front wheel was flat and the bumper had come to rest on the solid iron bar that, during the passage, had kept the vehicle from rolling into the Limfjord. Now neither the car nor the iron bar would move. We had six men trying to lift it at once, but it was a heavy car, and it didn't budge. We tried to use a hitch bar as a lever, but to no avail. The landing ramp was right there, and access to it was blocked by our car. For half an hour we maneuvered and gave orders but it was no use. No one reproached us for it but the mood was tense, and they avoided looking at us. Then it was all too much for one of the farmers. It was now or never. Grimly he climbed onto land, with the rope to one of the horse's bridles in his hand. He called to it, yelled and pulled, while another smacked the horse sharply on the rear with a cane. The horse danced and rose up, making the ferry sway. Then it jumped over the low gunwale and landed on the cement pier. The farmer swung around to the halter, until the horse was calm again.

After that it all went more smoothly. A primitive pulley was rigged up, so the horse could lift up the car's front end. We rolled across onto the pier, making room so the ark could be emptied. Silently they all departed, while the ferry shoved off and turned around for the return trip. A woman took the two young children under her arms, and one of the horses took the flatbed hitch bar under its arms, and away they all trotted towards the center of Thy, leaving us on the storm-beaten pier, with the water rising steadily. For the God-knows-how-many-eth time we took out the jack. It was worn out, and no one could blame it. The rounded teeth slid by one another, and for twenty minutes we took turns spinning the handle around, banging our knuckles against the cement. When we finally got the tire changed, waves were washing around our feet, and it was so dark we could no longer see the ground.

Then it became apparent that the car wouldn't start. We didn't waste too much time on this fruitless endeavor. Educated by experience and without unnecessary conversation we began pushing it inland off the pier. Fifteen minutes later we succeeded in depositing it beyond the sea's reach, and we climbed inside to spend the night. If we hadn't been so slow all day, we could have been lying in proper beds.

"Mo-clay," I said from the backseat. "A mo-clay factory!"

"Hamlet!" he answered, repositioning himself on the front seat. "Hamlet's *father*!"

"Relax," I said, since it was his car. "And stop yelling. Or we'll get a flat."

*   *   *

Translator's Note: Mors Island, 140 sq mi, lies in the Limfjord, the body of water that bisects northern Jylland, separating it from Vendsyssel, the tip of Denmark. Mors is home to a beautiful, diverse coastline that includes cliffs of mo-clay, a special type of diatomaceous earth, rich in fossils and in industrial uses.

A Journey in 1944

The doves' flapping retreat under the vaulted ceiling of the departure concourse, the send-offs from people on the platform, faces turned steeply upwards towards the passengers in the windows. *Send my love to them back home. Thanks so much for coming. Come back soon. No, next time you can come visit us!* A conversation that at the last moment rises to a frenzied crescendo at the second the doors are slammed shut. *Goodbye! Thanks so much! Send my love! Hugs to Auntie! Come back soon! Byyyyyye!....*

Wave, wave....

A young woman takes a few steps on the platform, still holding tight to her boyfriend's hand, which the train is about to carry off. Her face is dead serious. I watch her stop and wave and become smaller and smaller, then walk to the other side of the platform where she can be seen better, still waving. Finally she disappears, and I sense how she feels as she turns her back and, alone, walks up the steps of the train station, while the train puts kilometers and minutes between her and her boyfriend. She was wearing a little red hat and holding a handbag.

Why do I remember her and none of the others that were there?

An older woman in a tent of silver fox and holding two hatboxes forces her way through the aisle. She is both panicked and offended by the fact that she hasn't yet been able to find a seat.

"Won't you let me get by," she hisses at me, and I shrink to my thinnest possible form under her punishing gaze. "How am I supposed to get by," she says in the same tone to the next one, but he is a tall, traveling businessman, bright and imperturbable, who, in his own good time, collects himself to have a look at her.

"By moving your legs," he says, almost astonished.

"But there's a seat next to you!" she screams suddenly and pushes her way back towards him with her hatboxes.

"But that is mine," answers the traveling businessman.

"You can't take up places like that," she says triumphantly and is already past and about to remove his hat from the seat.

"Yes, you can."

"It says so in the newspapers!" With an ingratiating smile and pleading face she angles for agreement from others in the car, oblivious to the fact that they already hate her intensely.

The traveling businessman goes to stand outside in the vestibule—he can't be bothered to take part in this any longer, leaving it to the others to explain the truth of the matter, and get her out. They do. We can hear her demanding voice from the next car.

Five minutes later she comes back from her fruitless hunt. Attacking with her hatboxes, she fights her way resolutely through the aisle.

"I don't care. I won't stand for it." she says, ripping the businessman's fedora from the seat, smacking it down angrily on the neighboring passenger, planting herself heavily and adamantly in the seat, and continuing, without looking at anyone, to speak aloud about excessively gross inconsiderations.

Standing in the aisle, the traveling businessman stares at her with a faraway look in his eyes. Suddenly his attention piques, due to a terrible suspicion. He rises to his full height, with a smoldering look in his eyes and murder in his voice.

"Tell me. Are you sitting on my hat?"

The lady looks nobly away. The man, smiling, hands the hat out to him—intact.

"Oh, thank God," he says relieved, sinking back into his imperturbability, putting the hat on his head. "Then I will have to let the conductor remove you," he remarks to the lady and turns to leave again.

"You can be sure, that in another country a gentleman would not make a lady stand," she says in his direction, nodding to herself. She got him there, and it might be a good thing that others heard it too.

"I wouldn't either, if it were a lady we were talking about," he replies, looking at her uncomprehendingly.

On a trip. Something I ought to do only when forced by bitter necessity. Tall rowhouses turn into low bungalow developments, to storage yards, to factories, to developments without buildings, with only isolated houses shot up like flowers of speculation from the fertile earth. Slowly we distance ourselves from the capital, slowly the public railway chill begins to creep into my extremities. I have layered myself with sweater, jacket, wool scarf and trenchcoat. While reading the newspaper, I feel my feet turning to ice, freezing solid in my shoes despite my thick socks. At the stations it seems that the train is also frozen in place. It stops for so long that it is startling when it finally starts up. I almost forgot what I was here for. I guess the conductor has too, for the cars start rolling slowly backwards towards Copenhagen. It appears that they need to find a more agreeable position on the tracks, maybe more room to accelerate, for whenever it gets moving again.

But the Express, the wonderful Express! How I drank a glass of dry sherry at the bar and hardly had time to wipe my mouth and pay before we were at the Great Channel ferry. And who even needs a sherry in the express train? *Here* is where there ought to be sherry—a comforter and a bottle of sherry! Now the chill has reached my knees....

The train is still stopped. At intervals I shift around in my seat, when suddenly there is a jerk through all the cars. It's the same trick you meet at certain restaurants. Just when you have reached the utmost level of hunger and impatience and are about to call the manager, the waiter arrives with a knife and fork—your expectations are buoyed and you calm down. Ten minutes later, when you realize this was just an underhanded trick, that you have been fooled, you then are put at ease by the arrival of a napkin.

It is raining as the train starts rolling. The drops whip against the berth window, blending with the coal dust, running in strange erratic courses down across the pane, preventing any view.

Across from me a lady is sitting with her legs intertwined in a brown, plain, woolen blanket. She's in her mid-forties, the tall, lean type, considered elegant at the turn of the century. A heavy heirloom of a bracelet is resting over her glove. She is sitting with closed eyes trying to sleep, her long pointy nose red with cold. Most people are sitting with eyes closed, have given up on any activity, are trying to sleep away their suffering. Only one man at the table in the corner window differentiates himself. He is working intensely, not wasting a second, writing, taking notes, looking in a book and taking more notes.

He has removed his jacket, as if it were a summer day, and hadn't we noticed? A couple of times he looks around absent-mindedly at us, and gets an even more smug look on his face. Hale, hearty and efficient. Second by second he is distancing himself from us, and he notices this with satisfaction. Once, unsuccessfully, he suggests opening a window, to let in the fresh air, and afterwards his halo shines even brighter.

Oh, I know you. I know you, my good friend! I know your type back from my school days. You warm yourself inwardly by rubbing your self-satisfaction against your sparkling conscience. If I weren't sick I would smash you in your satisfactory existential underpinnings and cause you to slink ashamedly along the walls of buildings for the rest of your life. What would you say if suddenly I got up, did two minutes of quick gymnastics according to a particular system, rinsed myself with ice cold water, gave a lecture on vegetarianism, demanded a cross-breeze and wrote three short stories before we arrived at Vordingborg?

But I am too sick. I am doomed by this creeping railroaditis. The cold has reached my heart chambers.

A hot cup of tea!

When I get up to go out to the aisle, people open their eyes, look sickly at me to check if I close the door fast enough, so not too many of the accumulated degrees of warmth can escape.

Berth doors closed everywhere. People hiding in their half-dreams behind closed eyes. One reading a book with a plaid blanket up to his neck. A bald man pulling his hat down over his head, trying to lean back and sleep with it on, cursing its shape. A suitcase where gloved hands are playing cards.

Please Leave the Toilet in the Condition in Which You Would Like to Find It. That's asking a lot. It would take several hours of hard work to comply with that request.

A glimpse of autumn forest, all of autumn's flaming colors zip past the window and a little white house sails gracefully by on a field farther away. A pine woods, black in the grey weather and with telephone poles' white chimes hurrying along the edge.

Trying to cover myself better with my coat is no help at all, because it is also cold as ice. The lady's nose has turned blue and her face is even paler. How many traveling businessmen will survive this winter? But it is the intention of the state railway to kill people. Like an enormous squid it covers the country. *Come into my ice cold embrace!* Healthy and red-cheeked you enter at one end of a rail line, and at the other end you are delivered as a corpse, frozen in sitting position.

A station with a restaurant. I charge in, order a bitters, a matter of life and death.

"We don't have any."

"What do you have, then?"

"Nothing. Lemon seltzer, maybe."

"Is it cold?"

"Yes."

"Are you sure?"

"It's been in the refrigerator!"

The Great Channel Bridge—an impression seasoned by repetition, but suddenly individualized, imprinted as a momentary picture, because I glimpse a tugboat with three barges sitting deep in the water, working heavily out towards the Baltic Sea. And I guess it made me think, seeing them struggling to make headway against the wind and current, while I glided above past them in a train to another destination. Or maybe I would like to think something, but couldn't and lost my breath because of something beyond words. And a short-circuit occurs in that second, in that flowing stream of impressions, and a momentary picture enters the memory's collection. Bridge pillars, steel girders, coastlines, the gray sky and sea, flat under the wind, is built up, is stretched out and straightened in perspectives around a tiny tugboat with three barges, no larger than beetles, seen from this height.

How did it look half a minute before I caught glimpse of that boat? I don't know. I can only know in general how the Great Channel Bridge and the Great Channel look.

A strange combination is the remembered and the not remembered. The steady stream of impressions from the beginning of a journey until it ends—and the journey can be from the cradle to the grave—what sticks and why? What disappears, and what is incorporated in the memory's kaleidoscopic collection? Everything is seen, only a glimpse is remembered. The light continues to shine only on fragments.

Late in the evening after a trip in 1944 I arrived at a private train station on Lolland Island. I phoned the closest taxi. It couldn't come. I called other taxis, and finally reached one that could pick me up in an hour and a half. So I walked down a muddy path in the dark to a community center they had told me about at the station. The wind howled over the flat fields, the trees along the path creaked and groaned over my head, and it felt strange to think that they had stood there all day without moving at all. I entered the dark, damp community hall and felt my way between tables and benches. Then I knocked on a backlit door. A matronly woman opened and peered through the crack, then quickly slammed it shut again. I was just able to see her frightened eyes.

"There's nothing to be afraid of!" I shouted.

"Then what do you want?"

"I just want to get a cup of coffee or something to warm me up. I can drink it out here." I told her who I had come to visit, and why, and who I was. I stood there thinking of Blicher's stories.

The door opened a crack again, and she peered out at me, and I saw a sitting room with a plush covering on the table, and in the glare of the lamp some knitting and a wood stove, in front of which lay a little dachshund in a basket, plus a rocking chair with a pillow attached for one's head.

After she had had a good look at me, she said, "Well, I guess you might as well come in where it's warm."

Fragments of a Mirror

My father died when I was six. He taught me never to try to ride my bike diagonally over the railroad tracks. I can still picture it. I had gotten permission to follow him on my first bicycle, which still was a gleaming wonder, down to his warehouses on Esbjerg harbor. I remember the lighting over the expanses of cobblestones leading out to the North Sea and over the rust-red railroad tracks, where he instructed me. This lesson lodged deeply inside me, profoundly understood and accepted, a revelation of truth, and it made me feel more grown up. If he had lived longer he could have taught me other things that would have imprinted themselves just as deeply. I could have received more of the same satisfying security, the same pride. And maybe I could have learned important things about myself just by knowing him while I grew. Maybe by knowing him I would have been able to take stock of constellations inside me which now are just floating around in space.

I consider myself overly perceptive about other people. When I am not distracted by desires and emotions, sometimes I have the penetrating intuition of a fortune teller. But about myself I have no clarity. I am not even able to use my experiences to draw conclusions. Concerning myself all I can do is remember. And everything I remember, I remember in pictures, a film reel in my brain that recreates the forms, movements and lighting and underlying situations, not with words, but with moods. And the moods are so intense, that they have preserved everything except the sounds of words. They appear with humor, joy, sadness, excitement, all nuances of whatever situations between people can contain. I see people's long-gone facial expressions. I see the smiles around their eyes, the wrinkles on their foreheads. I see the lips forming words that were spoken years ago, so clearly that if I had the skills of a deaf person I would be able to read their lips.

When my father died we moved to Hellerup. I can't say that I had a remarkable childhood or that I lived in a world of fantasy. When I reached a certain age I dreamed about becoming a writer, but at that age my friends dreamed about that as much as I did. Of course there was a period in my youth that I wrote poetry, but there were several in my class who did that as well. With lurching ecstatic meter like in *Rungsted's Bliss*, we wrote comical lines about the teachers and the aides and about the other boys and girls. And they were a big hit, since we were at that age when both girls and boys are easily entertained by that kind of thing.

I can still see the girls laughing.

But that doesn't mean anything. My real childhood is remembered in another way. Usually I remember it as a summer with green leaves, sunshine streaming down between them. I remember it sometimes as a life in the summer treetops themselves, a strange atavistic memory. Was it ten thousand years ago? There were woods near our house, and we built hideouts up in the trees and down on the ground. We had bows made of ash wood that shot long and straight, and the arrows had either nails or knitting needles for points. I knew more about birds and animals and plants than I have known about anything else ever since. Our bows in our hands, from the treetops we could see boys walking on a road nearby, boys from another school. And it meant a tremendous amount to us, got us all excited, that we could sit there in secret and spy on them without being discovered.

We got to the hideout by a rope ladder that we could pull up after us. We were able get down another way on a branch that, when we clambered out, lowered itself enough for us to drop to the ground. Once a boy fell on his back and laid there on the ground with foam around his mouth and a rattling in his throat. It was crazy. His brother cried pitifully, and the rest of us figured that he probably had broken his back and was going to die. Half an hour later he was running around like nothing had happened, though still a bit pale and an object of our interest.

When I think about my childhood I am sometimes amazed that I survived it. It certainly would have been logical if some of us had been killed.

Once I was ski jumping in Deer Park and I landed on my head with my full weight, plus the skis. I don't remember anything after the fall.

That one part of my memory will always be impenetrable territory. I got amnesia. The first thing I apprehended was that I was skiing in a white wintery woods which I felt I had been in before through a previous existence. I was pretty sure it was some place in Scandinavia. I didn't know who I was or my name. I sat down on a tree stump, and there were animals nearby digging in the snow for food. Then some people came walking through the woods, and I noticed how they looked and I looked down at myself to see if I looked that way too. My perception of the lack of time and place brought on an amazement not unlike certain instances of poetic inspiration.

Another time, on a scouting trip, I was hit in the head by a hurricane lantern that had fallen from fifteen feet up. Perhaps that was the final straw that caused me to follow a writing career. It fell down from a flagpole and, obedient to its command, I collapsed unconscious.

I was the second-strongest boy in our class. That definitely does not make one into a poetic dreamer. And I was something of a phenomenon at swimming. I don't say that to brag. I mention it just to remember a boy that I long for sometimes, and with whom I have nothing in common anymore. When I entered the pool at the swim club, a whisper of respect traveled among the sunbathers, and my dear swimming instructor took out his stopwatch. When I was thirteen I swam the pool length of 33 and a third meters in seventeen and a half seconds. That is quite fast. But it is also a long time ago.

At a swimming demonstration for the school, one of our routines was for me to dive and lay down on the bottom of the pool. I could stay under water for a minute, and the other boy was supposed to pretend he couldn't find me. When the audience started to get nervous, he was supposed to bring me up and demonstrate life-saving and resuscitation. It went as planned. When I was brought to the surface, the principal remarked with relief from the other pool edge, "It's just pure laziness. He couldn't be bothered to get up on his own." The teachers around him thought that was pretty funny.

I had a reputation for laziness in school. Maybe it wasn't unjustified. My work habits in that world did have an absolutely sporadic character. I crammed for my exams and never did any work without first having to overcome my resistance to it.

I did get plenty of schoolwork done, but only if I weren't missing out on something else. As we grew older, I noticed that some of my friends missed out on things because they had schoolwork to do. Even long after I graduated I wondered about this. Even though there was something else more appealing, they chose to do work instead, without qualms, as if it were a natural thing. I felt astonished at this, completely paralyzed by surprise which reminded me of the feeling I had when I sat on the tree stump after my ski jumping accident. An astonishment that evolved into loneliness. It was such a life-altering realization and it made me so unsure of myself, that sometimes I put on an act and lied that I also had work to do that I wouldn't mind getting out of the way. All the while looking at them like I had looked at the people in the woods. Looking at them to see what they looked like inwardly. And afterwards looking at myself to see if I appeared the same way.

The first years that I studied law, I worked in an office as well. The people there were nice, we got along well, and I did my work without difficulty. Still I had a hard time because I had not yet learned what I would learn later. Earlier I had felt like my friends were slipping away from me because, in contrast to myself, they had decided to spend two-thirds of their lives on sensible choices which they appeared interested in. To me it felt that all of life was slipping away. I didn't even want to go to bed because that also stole life away from my freedom. Before I knew it I was going to have to get up again and then be cooped in the office. I spent evenings and nights on lonesome bike trips around North Sjælland. When I got home, I still didn't dare go to bed. Sometimes I didn't sleep for several days in a row. I parked my bike and went walking with my dog until morning. And there were the treetops and the clouds across the sky and the birds and the animals—everything I thought I was about to lose. So sometimes I would sit myself down on a tree stump and attempt to fix in my notebook some of that life that seemed to be slipping away. Then I could go to bed. Then it didn't bother me anymore.

When I wrote my first book, I often thought about my Danish teacher. He had opposed me with red marks that, added up, became my poor grades. A couple of times, when he read our grades aloud, he said that he wasn't going to give my essay a grade. I had interpreted this as an expression of particular hopelessness and from that perspective it didn't pique the interest of my friends or myself. When we graduated he came and asked me what I wanted to be.

"A lawyer," I said, and he shook his big bald head.

"That'll never work out. It would never be entertaining enough for you."

"Sure, it could be a lot of fun," I answered stubbornly.

"No, it won't be fun," he said. "But it is not unheard of that even lawyers can become writers."

"Whatever you say," I thought.

Then he stood there repeating: "Oehlenschläger."

"What a stupid, typical teacher thing to say," I thought.

He gave me his hand with a smile that seemed like an apology for all the red marks, and we said good-bye.

By the time I wrote my first book, he had died, but I thought about him because I understood that perhaps he had meant something else.

The fruit trees were in blossom at the time. I always remember what the surroundings were like when I wrote my books. From that first book I remember that there were cherry trees and an apple tree flowering outside the window, and that the apple tree still had its blossoms when I was finished.

A Man and His Great-Grandfather

How many city dwellers can count back a couple of generations in their family and not end up out in the country? Only a few. Some know where such and such a farm or such and such a place where their ancestors lived is located. Others don't. Some never gave a thought to where or whom they originated from. It's totally irrelevant for a city dweller where or who his forefathers might have been. What matters is work. Everyone is making their own way, just by hanging on. The heavy-set trolley driver, driving his car through the city's traffic, is he longing for the old fields? He doesn't give them the time of day. As long as the farm blood is pulsing in his veins, he is not thinking about it. He's content to make use of it.

And then one day you stand in front of the house where it was.

One day I happened to stand in front of mine. A random memory popped up while I was riding my bicycle through a country town. Wasn't it there that a deceased aunt once said…. And a church record allowed me to follow the trail further.

Then there I was, going door to door like a beggar, between the low thatched roofs of farms and houses spread so widely apart over sumps, heaths, and stretches of meadow that it was difficult to believe they were classified under the same name on the map. Mongrels yapped at my heels. A hand held fast to a door that was opened and the entryway was blocked by a body and polite suspicion. Who is this stray city chap? I also got a glimpse of a solitary heath drama. A young woman with a well-placed black eye opens the door. Her reluctance is not minimal. It was there beforehand. She opens a door to her bitterness and slams it again, as if expecting that I would slug her too.

It is the season when heavy red-striped bedclothes are hung to bake in the sunshine. Between the patio stones, weeds are sprouting, and pigeons coo pleasantly on the roof. A farmhand is standing high up on a cart full of heather, unloading. Politely, he averts his gaze after looking me over, and keeps working, as if that is the only thing he is occupied with. It's just a guy from the city. His reticence is like when you see a dwarf and of course don't notice anything unusual about him.

He shouts my question to another, half-embarrassed on my behalf: "Someone is asking if there is a place around here where someone named so-and-so once lived."

"Who's askin'?" shouts a woman from inside the house.

"It's a man...a gentleman." And he stabs the pitchfork into the heather to emphasize that I should not read too much into this. It is just the characteristic of an appearance, an outfit. The mannequin outside a department store is also a gentleman. As far as...

"What for?" she shouts from her hiding place in the house.

But he wants nothing more to do with it. He lets me field the question myself, if I want.

And I explain to him what this means to me, but he is unable to say it out loud. He opens his mouth a couple of times to repeat it to her, is the epitome of courtesy. But it cannot be repeated. Miserably, he goes back to working. He would rather crawl into a hole.

Eventually I am asked inside. A man in a homespun frock coat and slippers—an old man with a liberal flapping tie and low, crooked collar—approaches to receive me. I am invited to sit in the family room at the glossy, varnished, mahogany-colored dining table. Table doily and blue flower vase. Highly-polished, factory-made sideboard with a silver top. Clever businessmen have trawled the Danish countryside, and for ten-dollar bills tricked the country inhabitants out of these authentic and dignified old pieces of farmhouse furniture. But look at the man in his slippers. There is something the hustling agents could not buy, no matter how much they might have offered. Personal dignity. They drove off with antiques and dizzying profits, but the man kept for himself what was most important.

God help me if this man doesn't have a bearing that would make a diplomatic corps jealous. And without the least outward means—just the oak boards in his possession and his consciousness. No smile, but no undeserved suspicion either. A faraway look in his eyes, just after offering me his hand. But at the same time a respectability that is somehow contagious. I sit down to present my application to this minister of these foreign lands; I am no slouch myself. He bows his head, ready to listen, creating simultaneously peace of mind and an impersonal distance.

And, yes, of course, he has information to give me, he knows which family I mean, and he can show me where the house is that they left behind. In the last year many of the farms have ended up in the hands of families of strangers, just like this one has. Otherwise it was always the same families—fishermen and farmers every one of them. Usually the families even married into one another. His own family has lived on this farm for several hundred years. If the man I'm describing was my grandfather, then at some point far back we are actually related. He relates this information like the coincidence it is, and without his distance or impartiality lessening for a moment.

And was there anything else he could offer me, now that I am visiting the home of my ancestors? No, there wasn't. And he trades his slippers for a pair of clogs, and in his frock coat the old former fisherman and farmer follows me outside, a short distance down the road, until he can point out the particular house.

I will never forget his eyes.

It can happen that a city dweller, in a distant region of the country, meets the facial expression of his family among strangers. A pair of eyes, for example, that he suddenly recognizes.

They were my father's eyes that man was walking around with.

Big blue eyes that somehow had an independent life separate from his. Contact with them was only made on occasion, and that gave them a remoteness. He used them only intermittently to see out of. When he spoke with a person, he only had to bring them into focus, to *see* with them, for it to be perceived as a warm courtesy.

A rural person moves to the city, sits in a room in an apartment building, and before long resembles a gentleman, at ease in the milieu, not surprised in the least to be able to find his own home among the honeycombs. And the subway and trolleys. If you don't like your home, then move through the concrete maze to a new one. The subway and trolleys are there to accommodate the rootlessness.

Parents and children and, at most, a couple of grandparents. Bright in front and dark behind. The consciousness reaches no further. The view is no better from the third floor.

And the ancestors are just a couple of generations back—the lineage, the forgotten ones, the ones left behind, the place whose location you might not remember anymore.

Sometimes it can be found. A coincidental remark, that even more coincidentally has taken root, a church register's yellowed pages, an old man, noble in his simplicity, who has not been moved from the thousand previous years in himself, who has his roots well-preserved, who in any case knows what he knows, and does not pretend to know any more than that.

And there the house stands, the place through the many hundreds of years where nothing has changed. Its three sections huddled together, an old thatched roof, and low walls whose red bricks have been blackened by sun and wind. A single rosebush against the wall and also a garden in front. Sitting inside the rooms looking out of the windows, your nose would be at the height of the tops of the potato plants outside. In there they did their time, century after century. Blue and green glass balls, the kind fisherman use, are placed around a little garden bed. In the distance I can see that farmhand, standing in the cart of heather, working his pitchfork—in ten years he will still be there. The thatched houses and farms are spread across a square mile or so of the scraggly heath. On the telephone wires the swallows see-saw in the wind, and on the other side, only a hundred yards west, the cliffs stand like a mountain range, and the North Sea sounds its organ tone against the beach.

So it actually was my great-grandfather, the last fisherman and farmer of a long line, who lived here.

And time has stood still ever since. Here.

He brought in a bit of grain, but more fish than grain I'm sure. He also had potatoes to go with the fish, a single cow and a couple of sheep as well. And you can still see the sheep grazing behind the house. They have survived everything. When he got old, he was like the old dignified man I spoke with. Had no reason to be otherwise.

But one son became a livestock trader with more money in his greasy wallet than had passed between the hands of all his forefathers put together. The earning potential of previous generations accumulated and gathered in his pockets, just by his drinking an Irish coffee or slapping a man on the back. And on top of that the culture, the children's future, city life.

His son is not going to be a livestock trader, but a grocer or a wholesaler!

This is how people come to the city.

And a man, who could never bring himself to slap another person on the shoulder, who could not be *bothered* to have a drink in order to receive a product, to grease the skids, and who was distant to those he spoke with, became a merchant, bought and sold products in which he was not interested, to people he did not care for. He sat in the evening, reading books about animals and plants. City life. Every Sunday he took his children to the park or the harbor, made small, warm, awkward attempts to get them interested in single blades of grass or in the birds and animals. He could lift up a flounder and tell them everything about it. First, a flounder is of course not flat. It is compressed.

The children show no interest.

Two men, who one at a time traveled farther and farther from home, made it in the world, as you are supposed to as a city dweller.

And then it can happen that a third or fourth or fifth generation city dweller one day finds his way back to his place of origin, stands in front of it, looks at the same view that had been his family's for many generations. And the swallows are see-sawing on the telephone wires, the wind is whistling, the sheep grazing between sedges and lyme grass, and there are bluebells at the road edge. Time takes care of itself here. You don't have to help the time pass. It just stands still.

There I stood so strangely irrelevant and foreign. Like a highly polished piece of city furniture from the factory dropped at the roadside. And I don't own that place, which otherwise always was ours.

I sat for a half hour looking at that house, which had nothing to do with me anymore, imprinting on my memory the view to all sides. The sheep almost grazed the life right out of me by their ease and sense of belonging.

But I did realize a couple of things. I have very ugly hands. They are almost as wide as they are long. They were made to hold an oar, or to work as a livestock dealer, boring my fingers scrutinizingly into the tenderloin of a steer. They nearly cover the typewriter. And I often make mistakes.

It was as if these hands had come home again.

The Horse on the Beach

Down by the water's edge at the foot of the cliffs lay a dead horse. Sometimes the water washed up around it, but when it was low tide it lay high and dry on the beach stones. A light-colored horse. Or it could be it got bleached over time. I was living in a little house up on the cliffs during a few late, cool, but otherwise beautiful autumn weeks, and the horse lay down there the whole time—it lay there in the evening, as long as I could see, before the dark took over; and it was there again in the morning when I got up.

When I woke in the morning I was always cold, even though I had on several comforters, and it was a victory to get myself out of the bunk, stick my feet in the cold slippers and enter the dark, comfortless living room. The curtains were closed, and it got even more depressing when I opened them and the light revealed the mess from the previous evening. I lit the wood stove and put on water for coffee, and that helped a little right away, as if I had a kind of company at least. Then I went out to the faucet behind the house and washed up, which woke me up on the outside. I slipped on my clothes, gathered the mess on the table into one pile, emptied the ashtrays, put everything that made the living room appear untidy into the bedroom, shut the door, made the coffee, drank it, and felt that I was also beginning to awake on the inside. So I prepared myself: I poured a new cup of coffee, lit a cigarette, then opened the dutch door on the front of the little house.

And there it was. All of it. The water's limitlessness exposed, the cliffs stretching to the one side, and to the other side the little fishing village with harbor, jetties and roofs of houses. And below the cliffs the stones on the beach, then the larger stones that stuck up over the water farther out, and, down on the left—the dead horse. The water and the sky could change their appearance, but otherwise everything was the same. The same colored rooftops in the same relation to one another, the same lighthouse jetty turned in the same direction towards the water, the same cliff with the same profile, and the horse—of course it hadn't moved either. All of it the same, morning after morning. And yet, every morning it was new! Every morning a surprise, a dazzling novelty, just by its recognition, far exceeding what I had expected, correcting and supplementing the memory in a thousand ways, long after I was already satisfied. It was a revelation, a cleansing of the soul at this dazzling mastery in immutability. It felt so strong that I had to hesitate with my hand on the doorknob before opening, to kind of collect myself for what I was about to meet. And every morning the thousand sights were there again, like children who had yelled, "Come and look! Don't I look nice? I bet you can hardly recognize me!" But instead, it was, "Come and look how I am still the same! You had almost forgotten about me, hadn't you?" And every morning there were more things to recognize than I had remembered. And when I looked at them, they acted as if nothing had happened—a little game they played with me.

I hung over the half-open dutch door and a deep peace came over me from outside, brushed my head like the gentlest breeze. All the world's harmony strutted around like a possibility, like a truth stretching itself in thankful well-being, lying on the cliffs, resting between the stones on the beach, letting itself be washed away in the glints of sun on the waves, or driven away with the clouds, growing on the steep slopes, acting as if it were nothing, being completely self-sufficient.

My fingers noticed that my cigarette was burning all the way down. And the feeling that the typewriter was ready in the room behind me, and that the table had been arranged and prepared, that I had no more excuses, gathered itself with increasing intensity. And I tried to pretend like I didn't notice it, concentrated on pretending it was nothing, tried to light a new cigarette with the old one without thinking that I was doing it, looked down at the horse simultaneously, its body arcing up, all four legs stretched out meeting together. Its head lay among the stones in deep relaxation, but the tail was completely without hair as on a scrawny dog.

A couple of times it was precisely this which had been my big surprise. When, overwhelmed and nearly satiated, I had looked out of the dutch door on everything there was to see, my vision wandered across the beach and ended shocked. The horse! On top of it all—the horse! I had almost forgotten. And precisely with the neck and head down between two certain stones and the forelegs crossed in a particular way. Itself a piece of artwork in its entirety. The dot on the "i" of all this masterful abundance. I felt as if I had been, with a discreet but expert wave of the hand, made aware of precisely this finishing touch. I guess, you could say, it spoke for itself.

It made a much stronger impression on me than when I had first seen the horse. Then I just thought that it must have been a loose horse from the fields above that had fallen off the cliff and was killed on the stones below, but the fishermen in the inn didn't think so. When I had coincidentally talked about it, they had no idea there was a dead horse there. It had probably washed ashore, could have come from very far away. And they told me that once an old dead horse was dragged out into the water down by the harbor with a couple of ropes that they had tied onto the legs. And some time afterwards there was an article in the newspaper about a horse with bound legs that had washed ashore on the opposite side of Sjælland. Who had drowned that horse? The paper would sure like to know! They chuckled and shook their heads and rinsed it down with a beer. But they finally decided that it was repulsive that there was a horse lying there. It really ought to be pulled out at high tide. Sometime.

Of course the thought had also occurred to me that this could be the same horse that, outlawed and unwelcome on all the beaches, accusingly had returned to the place where responsibility for it lay. But not so much that I had been down to look to see if there were rope around the legs. On this count the thought would suffice, and it couldn't amount to anything anyway.

This talk about the horse got the fishermen to recount experiences having to do with death and horror that had occurred there in the village, where the colored roofs lit up for me every morning. The first one was about a man who had lain dead for so and so many months in an attic, until something about the flies in the skylight had led people to him. And then something about a man who was found hung in a vacation home. And the fisherman who told the story was there himself to help cut him down. He said the doctor had come in and felt the man's leg, determined its stiffness and said that he had been dead for several days; nothing could be done. But then he, the fisherman, said to the doctor that, regarding that leg, the man could have been dead twenty years because it was a wooden leg he got in 1920. And two hours ago he had seen the man in the store buying cigars. And did I notice the young man who had been sitting over there in the corner at that table the night before? Yes, I had. He was a fine-looking young fisherman, still at that age when they come home from the sea, and with long strides walk across the dining room floor of the inn, sit down and with a hoarse voice demand a coffee and two slices of layer cake.

"When he was six years old he was home alone with his mother, and the mother left the living room and went out to the washroom. The boy heard a strange noise from out there and when he went to the washroom, he saw his mother hanging from a rope she had attached in the corner. And the boy had enough courage, enough drive, enough rambunctiousness to cut the rope, a heroic deed, the ultimate rescue, but not enough sense or strength to loosen the rope around her neck. Instead he ran, wild with terror, over to his aunt who lived in a house nearby. But when he got there, the aunt had a visitor, a woman she was chattering away with. And the boy couldn't bring himself to interrupt and say what he was doing there. He stood waiting, staring up at them probably with a finger in his mouth. And when the visitor was gone they went back, but it was too late. Yeah."

But every morning the view spread itself just as peacefully and just as curatively outside the door of my house. No sorrow, no worries, nothing at all as long as I could just hold on, as long as I could defend just standing there. Small things could extend the time and be welcomed. Two children three or four years old in sweaters and knit pants were on an outing to the cliff one morning. On forbidden ground apparently, since their nanny stood somewhat perplexed behind the stairs leading down to the beach. But the boy was of course, a boy, though he wore glasses, and I think he was a few months older, so he dared to stand on the top step and at intervals go farther down, until his final cry of joy down on the beach, where he picked up a stone and threw it out in the mirror-like water with a plump.

"You put a hole in the water! You put a hole in the water!" she yelled, curling herself up with joy.

And he turned his little near-sighted face up towards her from the beach and his glasses gleamed superciliously.

"It will smooth out again," he said like a grown-up. And he already had a new stone in his hand, ready to give it another try.

I laughed out loud and calmly turned towards my typewriter, standing on the table with all its white keys. Yeah, go on and show your teeth, I thought superciliously. This here deserves an extra cigarette. It will all work itself out!…Ha! Two little hand-knitted tots at the world's ocean.

Another time I had stood and passed the time with a fishing boat that was on its way home.

At first a tiny dot far out, but now it was almost all the way into harbor. How could it make it if I didn't keep an eye on it? The fishermen out there suddenly turned the boat, sailing diagonally out again. They had caught sight of some ducks, out on the water, that they were attempting to get within shooting range. And the ducks flew off, alighting farther away, and the ship changed course again, chasing them diagonally in towards the cliff. For a quarter of an hour they stayed out, veering inanely in every direction, playing big ship chases a couple of ducks, which again and again flew away in time, before finally getting tired of the game. Then they flew so far away that the fishermen gave up and turned towards home. And I stood there feeling thankful towards the ship, in love with it while it lasted, in love with the mood on board. A ship like this, sailing home on placid water in the early morning sunshine, with everything organized after the night's work—the net hung up to dry on the mast, the deck washed down and rinsed clean, the ropes coiled up neatly, the smell of oil and saltwater—the way it is out on a ship like that, the sun reflecting on the water and glinting in the wet deckboards.

And as they sailed back in, I could see the people on board. I lifted my arm and waved, and they waved back. There was the captain, who had lodged himself comfortably behind the wheelhouse with his elbows on the roof, pipe in his mouth, and a foot on the tiller; another fisherman who stood in front, leaning against a backstay; and a very young man lying with his rear end in a rope coil and his legs over the railing. Together they let themselves be led through the sunshine in utmost ease, while blue smoke rings snapped upwards through the exhaust pipe. The boy slipped his one hand behind his neck to support his head while he waved. And when they came closer I could see that it was him—the young man who had been sitting in the corner of the bar at the inn. It made me want to embrace him, to be good to him, and it made me delight in these moments of sunshine, ship, and brotherhood even more.

I stood in the dutch door, taking it all in. I decided that even my restful horse deserved a thankful nod.

Sleep

I was traveling steerage across Kattegat, either because the cabins were all taken or because I couldn't afford anything better. My vacation was coming to an end. The steamship listed toward the wharf as people stood there, waving goodbye. When the ship emitted its satisfied roar to the heavens, the parting crowd crescendoed ecstatically for a few seconds. Handkerchiefs waved in the air, and emotional faces emitting deafening shouts turned towards one another across the narrow strip of water between pier and ship. I stood there waving a long time. Then I just stood, watching the coastline glide by. A couple of other people still stood there too, waving to someone who was probably also standing somewhere, waving back.

Then I walked the deck. I noticed a young girl in a bright summer jacket. She was the prettiest one there, and she was walking the deck too. Midships on the hatch were two students who had taken out a gramophone and were playing music. In their proximity lots of people were milling around. The young girl in the bright jacket placed herself midships at the railing, and the students stole glances at her. But with her back to them she stood peering over the water, keeping wholly to herself.

Below in steerage, older people had settled in. Across all the benches, quite a few people were draped, mostly older women, some already lying down and completely white in the face, even though it was smooth sailing. Others were sitting at the tables, drinking coffee and beer, and at a couple of tables the mood was festive and irrepressible, with sharp outbreaks of laughter declaring to everyone that here, cheerful witty people were enjoying themselves. Up on a comfortable luggage rack a young man lay looking out. You could tell right away, that when he came on board he had placed himself there to have that spot to himself. He had coffee in a thermos and a packed lunch, but he ate it laying down so no one would take any of his space if he pulled up his legs. His drawn face and bright eyes made me think of a certain kind of boys that I remember from school, self-satisfied and sophomoric in their kingdom of bagatelles, all of whom became engineers. You could see how he was relishing the foresight which had prompted him to secure his spot, and the prudence which he had employed to avoid paying for the ship's coffee, which moreover, was no doubt worse than what he had brought.

It was nightfall on Kattegat. Out in the fresh air, inside waterproof sleeping bags, fourteen boy scouts had lain down on top of the hatch in a row, like ammunition in a belt. Below, in the tobacco fog and beer-scented air of the steerage cabin, an elderly couple sat upright, sharing a blanket across their shoulders without a word passing between them. Their faces gave the impression they were awaiting a great calamity. They were still sitting there like that at seven o'clock the next morning. An older mother with her youngish daughter and the daughter's three small children lay in a corner on the hard floor. The one child, a boy, lay on his back sleeping a quiet, deep sleep. The second, a girl of about four, was sitting up with bare feet and big satisfied eyes eating a cookie. The third one, a girl of about three, lay on her back crying. She turned over, cried some more, kicked her legs, and cried even more, completely bright red in the face, nearly drowning out two other children that were crying in the room.

"Come over here and go to sleep. Otherwise we won't be able to go home and see Papa tomorrow."

"Come eat your cookie. Otherwise you won't be able to go home and see Papa tomorrow."

"Don't spit out Grandma's good chocolate. Or else you won't be able to go home and see Papa tomorrow."

A couple of hours passed in this way.

A man wandered around with five folding chairs and, in the end, placed them at a restaurant table. He then busied himself for quite a while with setting them in proper relation to one another, getting them even, and placing a blanket that he could wrap around himself. When he had tucked himself in, the blanket around his back and underneath him and his arm inside the blanket too, the waiter came and told him that he was in the way, and couldn't he see that this was no place for him to lie down. The man got up without a sound, but with a disturbed look in his eyes. With three chairs under one arm, two under the other, and the blanket over his shoulder pushing his hat askew, he shuffled off to find another spot. Nothing else registered with him. Sleep was chasing him around in a desert of unreality.

"Behave yourself and don't kick off your blanket. Or else we won't be able to go to Copenhagen and see Papa tomorrow morning."

The little girl had gotten quiet. With her face flushed from crying, she lay there upset and hot, kicking off the blanket with her bare feet.

At every location in the big room, wherever possible, people lay sleeping or without yet having fallen asleep. The lights were dim, and a sweetish smell from the cargo mixed with the tobacco smoke.

Only the most resolute were left. On a wooden bench by one of the tables sat a tidy woman in her thirties. She was dressed in black silk, stretched smooth over her full and somewhat spreading appearance. She was playing solitaire.

"You have to make the time pass somehow," she said cheerfully. It appeared that she was intent on playing solitaire with the same cheerfulness for the remaining eight hours. She was a vivacious young lady.

Half an hour later she was lying on the bench on her back, under her coat, turning a blind eye to both vivaciousness and youth.

An older gentleman, with whom she had been chatting, had replied to her that a trip was just a question of quantity of tobacco. He was going to stay up as well. He held his open newspaper like a man of the world. They were both superior to common corporeal sleepiness. About an hour later, bleary-eyed, and completely indifferent to everything and everyone, he removed his boots. With them in hand, he staggered over to a corner and snuggled headfirst into a pile of tarpaulins to hibernate. In his socks he kicked comically at the slippery floor as he settled himself. The only trace remaining of this man of the world in steerage was a pushed-up trouser leg and a purple sock garter.

That's the way it went for even the most obstinate ones who had waved goodbye at the pier. First a stiff, wide-open facial expression, followed by closed eyes, sitting upright for a few seconds, and finally, an almost panicked inventiveness as soon as the surrender had taken place. Some crawled up on top of luggage in the racks. Others lay under the benches or up on the tables. People snuck off to out-of-the-way corners and curled up to sleep like dogs, as reality fell completely away.

At one particular table, where some people had been making the greatest commotion, demonstrating their superlative vitality around a battlefield of beer bottles, all was now quiet. The last one left, sitting there all alone, nodded three times. And as if he had been shot in the back of the neck, he banged his forehead against the tabletop, and slept.

The one who kept herself alive in the cabin for the longest period was the pretty young girl. On the table in front of her she had a magazine, a box of cigarettes, and a compact. She had laid her fine, bright jacket carefully to one side. She sat, legs crossed, with a regal, elegant attitude, blowing smoke out her pursed lips. Something unconscious within her demanded that she keep herself awake, that she not give in to coarseness and lack of control. The minutes ticked away at a snail's pace, grew into years. I went above for some motion and fresh air. I could see the lighthouses blinking from passing islands. The starry sky was gorgeous, and the ship added its own gleams to the night as we sailed. But it was difficult to ascertain if this was any of my concern. There was another world inside me that was far more inviting. It was an ocean, larger than the one we were sailing on. An ocean of tiredness and rest, which I longed to fathom.

An hour later, I saw the young girl lying at the foot of a stairway in the middle of the damp, hard runner, in an open, windy corridor. She probably had sat on the stairs first. In her delicate, bright coat, she lay on the dirty rubber mat. Her mouth was open, and she was pale as a corpse, lying there asleep.

I went below to find a blanket for her. Bottles and cups still stood on the tables in the weak light, but not a sound other than breathing, not a movement. The room itself was sleeping. It was like a battlefield with twisted bodies. Only the older married couple sat upright, staring straight ahead, as if in a trance.

Deep down below this lifeless cargo, the ship's screw droned with the eternal sound of sleep, as if it were omniscient, aware, and standing guard, as the ship sailed on.

Then I walked above to the upper deck and let myself fall unresisting into the bottom of a lifeboat.

The Weeping Beech

I assume it was the bell-ringer's wife who showed me around. When I rang at the door of the little house next to the red public school on the other side of the road, she came out, grey-haired and sweet, with a friendly smile. While children's singing filtered out of the classrooms, she accompanied me back over the road with the big key in her hand, and let me enter the church's gloom, where I stood for a moment with my head back in the moldy cellar air, as one does when entering an empty church. But she didn't look up; she was so used to it. She just stood there with the key hanging from her hand, keeping an eye on me, her friendly smile around her old brown eyes, ready if something should come up, but still discreet. When I asked about something or other, maybe the age of the church, because that was likely the only intelligent question I could think of, she answered me without being the least bit tiresome. And when I walked towards the altar on the red coir runner, she stayed behind with her friendly smile, and I got the awkward feeling that maybe she thought that I was going to pray. And I was sorry that I couldn't bring myself to turn my head, and in a loud voice ask something or other about the altarpiece, or say something meaningful about it. It was baroque with gold leaf and many colors. I knew people who would have said without the least hesitation, "Wow, that sure is lovely," or "Wow, that sure is peculiar." Or else they would have found the entire church praiseworthy, but the altarpiece terrible—a blemish on the rest. I stood thinking about how little I knew about that kind of thing. I couldn't even guess in what direction their statements would have gone. The altarpiece reminded me mostly of an arrangement by the circus performers The Stefansen Brothers—like a shooting gallery in a midway where if you hit the target, you would be rewarded with a lively mechanical rattling from the whole installation: the angels would come alive, drumming and blowing the trumpets. But, of course, I couldn't say that.

Actually I don't really like churches, neither as architecture nor as artifacts and definitely not filled with people. What I do like about them—what gets me to go into country churches when I have the chance—is that vacuum they surround me with, that quietude, that sense of bygone generations' bowed heads, that sense that here reality cannot enter. And when you come out again, you have to get used to the idea that you have a watch on, and that it is ticking.

She told me that in the old days this church had been used as a fortress. I knew that beforehand, but since I sensed that I had already rubbed her the wrong way, I pretended that I didn't know and, surprised and interested, I wound my way up a narrow spiral staircase that ended at the tower's outdoor balcony, as if it were a part of the fortress design. From there I saw what you would expect: rooftops, and the widespread landscape of Sjælland in autumn colors, but no enemies approaching. Then, like a leaf falling to earth, I wound back down the spiral staircase again, over the church floor, and we exited together to the churchyard, where the light and the low sun offended our eyes after the dim interior.

"That is where we sought shelter in troubled times," she explained.

"Imagine that," I said. Her brown, Wendish eyes, so common in southern Sjælland, revealed that one of her female forebears probably didn't make it to safety after all.

"Yes, that is where they sought shelter," she said.

I wanted to give her some money for her trouble, but she shook her head. She didn't want any payment.

I had been going around acting so phony. The nice bank smile—*thank you very much*. And then it turns out I ended up meeting a person with honest, helpful intentions. Into the bargain she pointed out, before leaving, that there also was a tree worth seeing. She said that people thought it was the country's largest weeping beech tree.

The weeping beech stood between old graves close to the church wall. It reached all the way up to the roof and all the way down to the ground, and sort of clothed itself in the down-hanging branches' sorrowful robes, a tragic female character in the great classic style, just before the curtain falls, when everything has been said, and when the living have buried their dead and nearly themselves, and their own hopes as well. This tree reminded me of Betty Nansen in *Mourning becomes Electra*.

The weeping beech, by the way, is not a special tree species. I learned this from a forester at another place in Sjælland, where they also had the country's largest weeping beech. "Nope, it's not a special species," he said. "It's deficient—just like some people—they're trees there's something wrong with. They lack vitality. Their life-energy is stunted, so they don't stretch skyward like all other trees and plants."

But isn't the same thing characteristic of the tragic moment, the tragic ending—the surrender, the disabling of life: the rest is silence.

And there is a lot of silence in a churchyard like that. The gravestones in all styles stand crumbling with their final and eternal statements, like witnesses daydreaming within the reach of their own evidence. *Born* and *Died*. A great truth in that. A couple of places a load of withered flowers is showing, and a fresh, glistening gilt under a new chalk-white dove shows that here is someone who has only recently arrived. And it will come regardless. It has come for so many. I stand here between yew and arbor vitae reaching back in the centuries. Here is a man who died in September of 1918. He started out in 1849, and by the fall of 1918 was up in years. Maybe he had taken his last walk down a country road in just this kind of autumn sunshine. Could be he got the Spanish flu.

"So, it's the Spanish?" he might have said to the doctor, lying with his hands on the comforter.

"Yes, yes it is."

"If only I could have stayed to see the ending," he might have said, and repeated it a couple of times: "Just to have been there for the end…" —and thought about World War number one, and words like Marne and Verdun and names like Kaiser Wilhelm and Foch were fresh in his ears. I see that five years later his wife followed him down; then she would be able to tell him about the League of Nations. The dates are recorded on a rough-hewn stone sticking out crooked from one corner of the grave. That's the way it was done at that time, here in this region. You can see it on other graves from the same period. The living live their lives a while and then they also leave their mark on the graves. Perhaps this particular grave-style was the result of the vogue of the era with diagonally slung pillows and divans arranged aslant out from the corners. In any case, this man did not receive a tablet with a dove or a granite column or an opened marble book. His wife wanted him to have the noblest possible. And people who knew him, who some time after the burial went to have a look, returned and reported that Ole Hansen got a crooked natural stone, and others nodded knowingly and understood what that meant.

Inside the shadow of the weeping beech lay even older graves. Only the stones remain. A small, engraved coarse sandstone with an inset, darkened marble tablet: *Here lie the earthly remains of—fmr. Slr. Kristian Jeppesen —* 1780, † 1874—and his fmr. Housewife—Anne Marie Jørgensdatter— * 1790, † 1818*—is what it says. A *fmr. housewife* and a *fmr. slr.* Does it mean Small landholder? seller? Maybe sailor? Or settler? And yet. In any case it is so former that it doesn't really matter anymore. Totally moldered with age I imagine him—so old, that in the end, he willingly let himself be led up here. In the end, with the retrograde memory of the aged, he was not able to remember much other than Napoleon and Anne Marie Jørgensdatter. He annoyed people with his bright-eyed toothless talk about them, so it was a relief to fold the pale fmr. working-man's hands over one another and lay him down there, where he immediately fell asleep. For them it was as if he were still babbling while they helped get him up here. He had gotten on their nerves with his doddery banter for so long. Now finally a person might be able to mention Bismarck without immediately hearing about a Mr. Danton…. Danton! Who was that guy anyway? He probably wasn't even sure himself. Just a name he must have heard.

And then he went down to her, his wife, who back then was younger than his grandchildren are now, the age of his great-grandchildren maybe. Anne Marie Jørgensdatter! The young woman somehow was made even more tender by her youth, because of the long time that has passed. She appears clearly in my mind's eye—Goethe's contemporary, though she never heard his name. "Yes, it is true, she was spared much," the other wives said as they clothed her in her last white gown. And the gravedigger began marking out the grave under the weeping beech. *Thus shall we all pass one day.* And they would, too. It was so true, what they said. If there's anything one can be sure about, it's that. Now they are lying under stones with *the mortal remains of* or *the dust of* or *loved and missed* or *rest in peace.* White doves look down on the years that were engraved for them, and that already are long past.

The gravestones impart the course of lives, the age of the dust, which generally speaking is about 70, the man usually arriving some years before his wife. Walking in a churchyard can make you quite adept at adding numbers together from either side of a century. 1866 to 1933—that is, of course, 67 years. There are small graves with headstones that originally were stones for a single person, but then others were added as footnotes in the space that was left. Plus, affluent large family graves behind granite posts and iron chains, where you almost expect to see a sign: Private—No Entry. A man with his stone, proprietor of this or that farm, *R. af D. p. p.*[1] *born* and *died* and *peace* in gold lettering; the wife with her stone beside him - her name, but also her maiden name, and the farm where she grew up. It lies all the way over in Jylland. So how did they meet one another? Perhaps he was a student in a national farming program at a property nearby. A son and a daughter-in-law and she is also *born* and there was also a farm for them, and a daughter who was matron proprietor of such and such on such and such a farm, and another; but only *born*, their name, and in a corner of the grave next to one another, each under a small stone—just *Aunt Elvi* and *Aunt Asta*, a short interval between their two deaths. And they were also passionately enthusiastic about Prime Minister Estrup's fierce viking spirit—and *peace* in gold letters with the rest.

What is it have they gotten peace from? The hundreds of acres that now are traded for seven small beds in the gravel?

Three shovelfuls of earth, a thump by the velvet hand of time, and afterwards resignation and stillness.

And then a place where the stillness is broken by a jarring incongruence. A boy who died at 18—an inexpensive stone, and below, the name and years. Neither *peace, sleep well* or *be ever cheerful*, but only in large letters: WHY. I perceive a conversation between the father and the priest on the occasion, the man sitting with bowed head, turning his cap in his hands. Is he sure he wants that inscription? It's not our lot to ask, we know only that not a single sparrow falls to the ground, etc., and who knows, perhaps it was best for the boy? Then why was he

---

[1] Chivalric Order of Dannebrog, praeter plura

even born? the man may have mumbled, if he could muster opposition. But maybe it was for him and his wife, the priest continued. Could it be that perhaps it was simply to test them? But I wonder if that wasn't making more of him and his wife than necessary, the man thought—a whole life in eighteen years. Couldn't his wife or himself have been taken and then tested the boy instead? The boy could have achieved so much that he himself could not. But he didn't say this. He just sat there, loathing everything. The *why* wasn't even so important any more, so exceptional—it had already given birth, had become multiple *why*'s, as questions are wont to do. Why had he, for example, not had enough money to send the boy away, so his life could have been spared. And why was he now forced to sit here and listen to all this prattle. He cleared his throat. Yes, of course, he understands that the pastor is right. It was just that, as the pastor well knows, the boy was pretty much the only thing we had....Yes and then this occurs.... But then in the end that came to be written on the stone, and he didn't have money for another stone, so it would have to remain like that after all....

So there it is on the gravestone. WHY. The most dangerous word in the world. The source of every change, each advancement, where every discovery begins, and which therefore shall be suppressed or indulgently smoothed over. Already in children's books we begin to quash it. The irritating, never-ending questions: Why doesn't a moo-cow have wings? Why wasn't I born a cat?

Probably similar to the same wondering that once took hold of Darwin...

A matronly woman passes me at the churchyard gate. She is in a hurry; she's been shopping. She goes over to a stand and takes a communal watering can from a hook. She does it mechanically, doesn't follow her hands with her eyes. While they reach for the watering can, her head is already turned away towards the grave, in the direction she is about to walk. Not even the sign—*Please return the tools to their proper place after use*—enters her consciousness. Everything is so familiar that nothing registers with her anymore. And then, as if her haste is suddenly dissolved, she walks casually among the graves to a certain place with boxwood or hornbeam or a wrought iron fence around it, where there is someone waiting for her, and where there perhaps is a little bench where she can seat herself and pause, looking at the headstones she greets like old acquaintances.

The sun is shining gently on the low houses on the other side of the road. The flower pots in the windows are low, close to the rough sidewalk, and the smoke from the chimneys rises straight up. The leaves of the rowanberry trees are nearly as red as the berries themselves. A blackbird sits uneasily up there. It is the only thing moving, lifting its head after each mouthful and looking around. Yes, now it is autumn. The berries are cool in its beak. Clear, open, long autumn. I lean my head back in the thin air, the sky is so far away and blue that I have to close my eyes.

Then I hear the singing again from over at the school. The children's voices through an open classroom window. They must be very young. A little girl, no higher than third grade, exits the building with a bag over her shoulder and takes a drink from the water fountain in the schoolyard. She catches me listening and flashes a roguish and understanding smile. Dear God, the sweet little ones. It sounds so touching! Sometimes the teacher's violin plays entreatingly beside the singers; sometimes he sings along himself, a baritone with a folksy timbre. When I can't hear him or the violin, it's probably because he is swinging the bow like a wand, and enjoying too, these innocent little ones. Honestly, it is deeply beautiful. It's easy to make children's voices sound pretty; they get caught up in it as well at a particular place they like, where there's an especially lively swing in the melody. They sort of put extra energy into the approach and then put all their strength behind it, so you can make out the words—if I hear correctly—*Be friendly and nice....* Verse after verse the children's voices ring together all through it, and with the same happy abandonment at precisely that one place in the melody—yes there is no doubt—*Be friendly and nice....* Must be a rather didactic song. When it abruptly ends I hear the teacher's voice extracting the moral, "Yes, *that* you should take to heart!" And the children laugh, enjoying the moment.

I wonder who should take what to heart? Who in the song is being reprimanded by that righteous reciprocity? Is it a director for a private capitalist weapons dealer or some other person who could be a danger to these children? A military dictator? A hypocritical powerful politician? I doubt it, probably not. As I remember from my own youth, it's probably just some little Hans who climbed up in a stranger's apple tree to steal an apple. But the branch broke and little Hans fell down and hurt himself and the strange man came out and gave every child an apple except for Hans.

I tear myself away, slamming the gate behind me, and continue out past thatch-roofed small farmhouses and red-gold stubble fields, where chickens are foraging. The sun is not the summer sun any more, which embodies the term sunshine. It has become a distant globe, retreating in space.

The silence, the clarity—yes, God help me—almost piety in such an autumn.

Be friendly and nice....

Dear God...Dear Anne Marie Jørgensdatter! Help the children, so, when they make it over there, to all the used-up people there in the churchyard, that they have used themselves well—that they have not let themselves be used or tricked too much. Deliver us from the grown-ups. Give us peace.

The Specter of Regret

Something I regret doing? A certain action—one I regret more than others—one I regret in particular? I don't know. In the lower grades of elementary school there was a boy we called "Smelly." And of course that couldn't have been too pleasant for him. I can still smell him. Once when we had to practice a song in chorus the music teacher put me next to him—a grouping I hope was undertaken only for musical reasons—and I refused to sit there, stood up demonstratively and sat silently with my nine-ten-year-old insulted dignity somewhere else. You can't make me. A moment's common surprise by the teacher and the students, but followed by immediate silence, discreet understanding. There was Smelly, sitting there with the empty chair next to him, a little boy forced into a pariah existence. The music teacher rapped her wand: "The Swedish national anthem—*Du friske, du frie, du fjeldhøje Nord!*"

I hope that teacher regrets not smacking me in the head.

My math teacher was a sweet and lovely woman. When I see in naive frescoes from the middle ages their detailed depictions of how ecstatic and how with such great preparations a lost soul is received by the demons in hell, it reminds me of her. That is how we received her. We had the tridents and glowing coals ready. And she was a lost soul, pale and kind of moribund—I can see that now. She had tried everything of course—tried with carrots, tried with sticks—eventually just stood there, rattling away with no one listening, writing equations and drawing geometric figures on the board. She had an aged mother and kept house for the two of them—we knew this, even at that age; but either we didn't quite get it, or it didn't matter to us. That was her business. Sometimes she would go blank and in her uncertainty make a mistake and erase it with the wet cloth and then make another mistake. Then she was completely lost. But from time to time the bubbling inferno behind her would subside and we became a calm, well-behaved class. That was even worse, and she kept on calculating with a voice slightly trembling. She looked down on us, ashamed, when it was absolutely necessary, and would not even glance at the door, since she knew as well as us, that now the principal's stern face was visible outside the little glass pane in the door. He had heard the noise again and thought he needed to debilitate us: the catastrophe that creeped closer.

This is how she went hour after hour from class to class until she ended up in a mental hospital.

And the meanest, the most reprehensible of all was when our sudden good behavior was pointed and demonstrative. Then they could both see, the principal and the teacher, how good we could be when the right whip was swung over our heads!

What had she ever done to us?

And then on the other hand: Is it something to regret? Why burden children with an unsuitable teacher? Why burden them with a responsibility like that? Actions will always have consequences. The same must hold true when action is not taken. You just have to break the spell—or the regret. Take heart, Antonius!

And still!

Aw! Ow! Ow! It can cut right though you, it can shriek through your whole nervous system—that time! and that time! and then that time!

A single action I regret? I have more like a regret schedule, a condition in which I meet it all, where I encounter nothing but regret no matter where I turn my attention. Maybe several schedules, each having its own level of contrition—differing perditions where I am beaten into martyrdom by actions and omissions standing by with their tridents and tongs. Come and get me you little devils!

It is not so much the really great mistakes in life that feel so entrenched in the end. They become assimilated as part of one's self. That Denmark had to surrender Skåne, Halland and Blekinge is not something you can continue to lament. It is just the way things are. It is the nature of things. But considering the limits defined by one's character and abilities—that you could have done this or that differently or left this or that undone!

Sometimes it can be completely irrational. You didn't do anything— and still! An apparition robed in regret is hounding you. Once as a new graduate I biked through Berlin to Paris, and at one of Berlin's intersections I braked for a red light, properly, like you're supposed to, and somehow something happened anyway. A little man who was rushing to catch a trolley brushed my front tire and started calling me names.

"And you can just watch where you're going," I answered.

"Watch where you're going! Watch where you're going!" he snarled from the trolley platform.

Then suddenly he jumped back down, ran five steps to where I was standing, whacked me painfully, and then jumped back up on the platform again where the conductor already had pulled the string.

"Watch where you're going," he yelled mockingly when the trolley drove by, and the other passengers laughed. I remained standing there, astride my bicycle with cheeks burning, in the Berlin intersection.

Something so inconsequential. Perhaps I had unconsciously violated some special Berlin traffic protocol. But I don't think so. I am actually sure of it. I have thought a lot about this since— that is what is so stupid about it. What I said to him—that he could watch where he was going—was also grammatically correct German. I was really quite good at German back then. So what happened? How do I know? But the beating ruined my day, cast a shadow over the forthcoming vacation, turned up like a burning feeling of shame. This was twenty-five years ago, but it can still turn up. My totally insipid gaping, their conspiratorial laughter. Just because I was a foreigner.

If I walked up to Saint Peter, it wouldn't surprise me if that little man were standing behind him. And they would both laugh before slamming the door, and the heavenly carriage would drive by.

"Let me in! Just for a minute!" I would shout. "Give me just ten seconds, then I can explain everything!"

Something I really regret? Something from when I had gotten to an age, a standing, when I really had a choice, a responsibility?

After I had been in Greenland, about twenty years ago, I was in the company of Greenlanders at a Christmas Ball or whatever you call it. In any case, there was dancing afterwards. There was a young Greenland woman and I had never seen anything like her, never seen anyone more beautiful. She was thin and fine like a very pretty Japanese geisha. I remember thinking of Anabella in the film "La Bataille." But it was a sacrilege even to compare her to anyone. She had the kind of beauty that ranks with genius. Suddenly there is a brilliance walking around like a light in the grey morass raised on high above the others, like the way Einstein is elevated over the regular masses of mathematics teachers. And you can't take your eyes away. I danced with her a few times. She was so light in my arms, she floated like a down feather from my bed-pillow when, as a child, I plucked one out and blew on it to keep it afloat.

"Any chance we could see each other again?" I asked her.
"Yes," she would like that.
"Could I call you?"
"No," she didn't have a telephone.
"So how could we make a date?"
I could make it whenever I want.
"Was she free this week?"
"Yes."
"How about tomorrow?"
"Yes."
"Where shall we meet?"
I could decide.
"Could you come over to my place tomorrow?"
She would like that.
I just had to tell her where I lived and when she should arrive.

I stood there. On a magic carpet suddenly laid before the entrance to a world of dizzying possibility. The music had stopped. I stood holding her hand and realized that everyone was looking at us, because everyone was always looking at her. I felt obliged to step back, because it looked like we were up to something. I arranged that we would dance the next dance together and I returned to my seat. When I passed the band, one of the musicians that I had gone to school with called me over.

"Who is she?" he whispered. "I can hardly play when she dances by." I just shook my head and sat down flummoxed with the others at the table.

"That is a very beautiful young lady you are dancing with," said a polar researcher's wife to me.

"Yes, very," I said.

"She is engaged," she said acerbically.

"Well," I said, unaffected.

"She's going to be married, but her fiancé is sick at the moment."

"Well," I said. Then it dawned on me. I had heard the story before in Greenland. She was from Jakobshavn. A geodesist had seen her and immediately proposed. Would she return to Denmark with him and get married? Yes, she would like that, she said, presumably. When? Well, he could decide. And she traveled to Denmark and in the meantime he had a long-term illness.

Considering these circumstances, it was clear to me that I ought to hold back. There was no way around it.

"You're engaged," I said to her, next time we danced.

"It's okay. He's very ill," she said. An innocent untouched by moral statutes.

But this of course did not acquit me in any way. I knew full well what morality demanded.

So I steered myself after these "dictates of morality." I achieved victory over myself. Go jump in a lake! The following day I could have opened the door and she would have been standing there in all her beauty, which now would have been directed towards me. And I could have taken her by the hand and led her inside, Indra's daughter, arrived on Earth to experience the conditions of humanity on their own level. Despite all this, not everything is regret. I still have delightful things to think back on. But she would have been a light in the tarnished corridors of memory.

That it never amounted to anything is one of the things I regret. It has become a ballast, a shame that weighs me down. I failed. Once I heard Bartholdy's Christian Evangelical Report on the radio and thought—*This I am not too crazy about.* But at the same time I felt embarrassment and shame. *Who are you who dares to cast the first stone?* I asked myself. *You have nothing to brag about. You were once moralistic yourself.*

But, as I said, only examples—and coincidental. Slag picked from an ashheap and set aglow once more. Hangovers. Like when someone the day after a party calls and says thanks for the party and apologizes for their behavior. Did they behave poorly? Of course they did, they are pretty sure of it! It was embarrassing. They realize that now.

Life's hangovers. The distaste of experience—the common man's remorse after *that party*. I have a feeling that if I had an awakening after *that*, my first thought in the midst of the dismay would be for a telephone, to call and ask: *Was I embarrassing? Was I that bad?*

Thirty Years Later

Thirty years later. After what? After I was young and wrote a novel called *In the Middle of a Jazz Age*, and now I am sitting editing it because a new edition is being published.

Thirty years after I was twenty. Okay; in a way this is nothing new, totally natural. I have had time to get used to it—to the situation. We simply *are*. Always have been. And now I really am fifty years old—fifty years that I sit with and expound from as if it had always been this way, as matter of fact as if it were perfectly self-evident.

But once in a while I feel a tingling in my hair roots—in those hair roots I have left—because actually it's not that way. It's not a matter of fact, not something to just be taken for granted, except in the most banal circumstances down between the dusty, musty scenery, where we play out our daily comedy from hand to mouth to avoid thinking about it, to avoid feeling the drama of age, down there where we are—if may I say so—at peace.

At peace with ourselves. At peace with who we used to be—at peace with our youth.

I have memories in the back of my mind—pictures—an album full. Only at certain compelling moments do I take them out. And I feel distant and strange while I page through them, trying to hide, from the people I am showing them to, how strange, how surprised I feel. That album which is called One's Youth—the closed album put away on a shelf. If it crosses my mind, I usually remember only one of the pictures it contains. There is a fourteen-year-old boy sitting on his bicycle, supporting himself with his arm against a post of the red gate by Hjortekær. The monastery grounds lie before him in the evening sunlight, his hair is like a sheaf of grain on his head in the wind at dusk. My youth. But I turn my thoughts away, don't give it another thought, maybe because I know that it will be uncomfortable—not entirely pleasant anyway. That boy doesn't know the fifty-year-old and the fifty-year-old barely knows the boy. And there is the risk of getting lost in the depths of the album—thousands of pictures, like a jungle to hack through, with no road or path. It is probably best to leave the album closed, put away. There is a fourteen-year-old boy sitting on his bicycle, supporting himself with his arm against a post of the red gate of Deer Park, and I turn away from him, think about other things, of the delimited moment, making a living, since otherwise he will leave the post and ride away. He's so young, so open, so alive, always ready, on his way, on his way where? On his way through life, on his way through the years. Probably felt like he was on his way towards something. Now I know better. Now I sit at the other end, there where he arrived, knowing that actually he was on his way *away* from something.

A Belgian doctor has put forward a theory about *biological time*. He based it on the difference in speed between the healing of injuries in young and old people. He made the speed of healing a constant, and time a variable in relation to this constant, and he reached this result or postulate: that already as children we have lived over half of our lives, half of our time. As a twenty-five year-old, we have used up four-fifths of our life, even if we live to a ripe old age. And when we get up in years we are likely to agree with him—with respect to our perception of time. Who doesn't remember how long a Sunday or a summer month could be when we were children, what possibilities lay in days, weeks, months? And who, on the other side of the hilltop, now on the way down, doesn't wonder about how fast time goes now, how the weeks fly by like days, the months like weeks, and how the years are gone before you even had a chance to look around. Childhood and youth were long. It can seem like those stages of life lie behind us like the childhood and youth of all humanity—a millennia-long prehistoric age. The dispersed pictures and memories we have from back then can feel like archeological discoveries. We stand with some unearthed memories in our hand and try to conjecture our way to something approximate, something close to how it was back then. Some of the discoveries are more valuable than others. They deliver a message, where otherwise all other connections had been severed, and they give us a glimpse of how it felt then to be alive. A boy of fifteen-sixteen who was visiting family in a rural town in Jylland—it couldn't have been too exciting, but everything probably was back then. Just life was enough, just taking a walk was more than enough, and he went for a walk alone in the company of his fifteen-sixteen years, but that was plenty. It was plenty just to walk, to take step after step and know there are many steps yet to take, that day and the days to come, an inexhaustible supply of steps. And he came by chance to a place along the road, and it was afternoon, which otherwise is the saddest part of the day. And the weather was nothing special—nondescript winter weather. It must have been Christmas vacation—no wind of any consequence; black, undulating, plowed fields; here and there a bit of snowdrift; sometimes a stretch of scrubby woods with loose snow sprinkled on withered leaves on the forest floor—and twilight already begun. His steps led him a few yards off the road up onto a little hill to take in the view. It was no impressive vista. A hundred yards away lay a sad, over-wintering plant nursery. But suddenly, with the winter air, breath after breath, he drew in a steadily increasing happiness, a harmony, a sense of belonging, a delight so intense that he could hardly bear it—a bright consciousness about the world that lay around him and the life that lay before him. Thankfulness. Gratitude. It was like being reborn. It was like becoming brand new for a few moments.

It was an inner experience of shock-like nature—so strong that it still stands like a rainbow over the hilltop, bringing a message from youth on the one side to old age on the other. Perhaps it is the only experience of that kind I have ever had, perhaps payment for an entire life and perhaps payment enough. I call it an *experience*. Several times when I have been in an intense situation of one kind or another for the first time, a life-changing watershed event, this word has come to me. A well-worn word with a completely new luster, an entirely clear and precise meaning, so that I somehow saw the word reborn, realized the situation that had created it, and perceived the psychological genius with which it was imbued. Once in distant times, in the infancy of humanity and language, a person stood still and looked around and wondered amazed at the happiness of every breath, at unbearable delight—a bright consciousness that for a few moments felt completely new—the self-awareness of existing. And it felt like a spasm inside him, like the unutterable—what there are no words for—can be, and he fumbled for some way to express what happened. And the word *Experience* was the result, a word for something big, for an initiation that could happen to people. And now it's just a simple little word—a word worn simple and smooth like a beach stone by the waves of language through the centuries. A word to put in your pocket. As a youth twice I had an *experience*. Later I had to settle for experiences.

The other one had the opposite indication. Then the circumstances were ripe for great pleasure. Twenty-five years old; a beautiful summer day. Together with a girl I liked I was lying on a beach in northern Jylland. We had just been in the water and were sunbathing under a mild balsamic breeze. Then suddenly I felt the crush of a weight—heavy, tragic, eclipsing, pressing into me, a deep sadness, arriving like a revelation—but this time about life's transience. It felt strong—evidently so strong that it was visible.

" What's the matter?" she asked suddenly. And the feeling was so overwhelming, so genuine to me. I remember that, totally slack, totally open, without caring that it could sound like some kind of comic nonsense, I answered:

"Time is going so fast. I feel so old...."

You can smile at it, smile at young people who feel "tired" or "old." feel like they have "tried everything." When you get older you put apostrophes around the feelings of young people. But still they can contain truth. A young man can feel that his life is almost over and be right. Because youth has only one life—*youth*—the rest doesn't count; not for them. Not yet. Johannes V. Jensen describes children in one story as "the little folk," expressing how they are people with their own world, cut off from others, are simply small people.

And youths—young people—are a people unto themselves. They feel that way, feel like the new arrivals, the conquerors—peacefully disposed, at least relatively, towards the natives, the land's older residents. They have strange customs and views, these natives, entrenched in their beliefs and superstitions. But leave them be in peace—they will die out all by themselves.

They will die out quickly because they are old. And we have time before us, we will always be young. That is the attitude of youth, the belief of youth, youth's security, whether it is in the middle of a jazz age or in the middle of a jazz club age. Of course we know with our thoughts and reason that we won't always be young—that we have to get old and die someday—but we don't believe it. We are still in the slowly inclining curve, haven't reached the top where we can see the downhill on the other side, falling away from us. Old age: the end at the bottom of the slide. Youth and old age, on either side of the hill top, cannot see one another, barely can contact one another. When I sat editing *In the Middle of a Jazz Age* I was however reached by a shout from the other side—my own voice—in a sentence I had once written, a tossed boomerang that had circled over time's peaks and hit me in the forehead. A girl, who is about eighteen-nineteen, is telling a man a couple of years older, whom she is in love with, that she is going to be married to a man who is well off. Because if she can't have the man she is in love with, at least she is going to have one with money.

"What is he?" he asks. And her answer should be imbued with tragedy, with all her bitterness, with the squandering of her life, now that she has sold herself and her youth for the sake of money. That since she can't have the one she loves, she is throwing herself away.

"Thirty-five." she says, staring out over the water...

And here I sit at fifty. Is it *so* bad? At first I thought of deleting the sentence, rewriting it, since it seemed so childish. But on the other hand, still—I decided to leave it.

Vanished Summers

One spring day a previous summer became real to me. I was going to show the house I used to live in to some people who were thinking of renting it. The house had stood empty over the winter; there were boards across the windows. The people walked around inside examining the large living room and the small bedrooms and whatever else was there.

"But where is the kitchen?" asked the wife.

I walked through the dim living room and the hallway and showed it to her. "There is also a fine, large cellar downstairs," I said. "And a maid's quarters too."

"It looks really nice," she said.

"It's a great house," I said. She stood staring down the cellar steps, and I recognized the smell. I looked into the maid's quarters to see how it looked. That was the only part of the house I had never seen before and did not know inside and out. The maid had lived in there. So that's the way it looked. That's what she made do with. A couple of times the maid had surprised us with warm apple dumplings in the evening. Once I came home from a bike ride and the mailman had been there with a certified mail cash payment for me, and she had signed for it, and handed me the money with the same expression with which she served apple dumplings—totally closed off from the nearly bursting satisfaction she felt to see other people happy. Once, when I had returned from the beach in my bathing suit and had gotten hot again, I got her to pour a bucket of water on me, which was much colder than the ocean water. And when she stood with the empty bucket in her hand and saw how much I relished it, she had the same expression as after the apple dumplings and the certified letter. When I walked away from her, I discovered with the first step, that I had forgotten to take off my shoes, that they were full of water. I walked across the grass with the wet shoes, too hot to take them off, until I was safely in the shade.

The yard was so strangely stark, seeing it again. No leaves on the trees or in the hedges—I could see right through them and far into other yards. Back then it was dense and blocked by green, like a world unto itself.

"That looks like a nice spot," said the wife, pointing between the pines to where there was a bench. The husband agreed.

No one ever sat on that bench. On the other hand there was always an empty playpen on the grass. Once a little girl was set down in it and she screamed and cried and whined through a morning and most of an afternoon, while her parents moved around inside the house, apparently upset and without uttering a word to one another. They had purchased that playpen so their daughter could be in it and get some fresh air without getting hurt. So why was she never in it? She didn't *want* to be in it! So she had to get *used* to it. She wasn't going to be raised believing that she could tyrannize *them*.

"There, you see," said her father, in the afternoon, when she had stopped crying. "Now everything's alright."

Five minutes later she fell asleep from exhaustion. She lay on the pillow sleeping in the mild weather, while birds chirped and small titmice fluttered around between the pine trees behind her. When she woke again, she got up on her knees and looked around. Her face clenched to a great wail. She stood up, recalling her misery to its full extent, and the screams resounded with renewed energy. Without giving the father the benefit of even a glance the mother walked out and picked her daughter up. After that the girl toddled around in the yard and in and out of the house's doors again, like she always had done; and ten times a day her mother had to rush out to the gate to retrieve her from imminent adventures out in the wide world.

Once I came riding on a big horse. After a fierce struggle I got it through the narrow gate and presented myself with the proud monster on the lawn. I thought it was quite splendid. Foam flowed in flakes from its bit, it quivered with nervousness, kicked and planted its back legs between the roses. The family congregated on the veranda. The father had the little girl in his arms. It was for her sake that I had come with the horse. She reached a hand out towards it—wanted to have it.

"Cheep cheep!" she said. She had learned to say this to the canary.

"I think we would enjoy having a bench like that," said the wife, still referring to the place between the pines that we never used. Her husband and I nodded affirmingly. I stood with my jacket, hat and gloves on in the open, windy yard and felt so alone and foreign to these people who were going to live in that house.

When it had been good weather, we went right from our morning coffee out to the yard, already in bathing suits, sat on the veranda steps or in a chaise lounge by the hedge with the wild roses and witches broom. Or we threw ourselves right down on the soft juicy lawn, hiding ourselves from one another with our newspapers in the sunshine until we were more awake and conversational.

Sometimes a memory can be so strong that you think it's the past which is real, and that the present is just an existence in a ghost-like condition. That house and that neighborhood suddenly permeated me with all kinds of weather and all hours of the day. Early summer mornings when I was woken by warmth and birdsong. Days when I snuck out in a raincoat to break off a collection of damp twigs and later sat reading for long afternoons by a fire in the woodstove with rain on the windowpanes. Or when I worked in my sweater and overcoat. You can stand there, eating cold, rain-soaked red currants off the bush, while the sky is a dizzying mountainscape of clouds in motion, or you can eat sun-warmed red currants in the company of buzzing bees and flies. But it is not until you never eat red currants anymore, that it actually feels real.

There were evenings when I rode my bicycle out through golden fields of grain, chewing on a seedhead of fresh wheat, kicking reluctantly on the pedals when the sun had long since gone down, yet everything was still bright. There were little dogs, white-washed small farmsteads, a harvester lifting its one wing towards the evening sky, and the air's coolness was like healing medicine on my skin after a day in the sunshine. And there was an evening when we were soaked through and ice cold after two hours of riding on the motorcycle—so wet that our shoes gurgled. Finally we made it across the garden path, and I was so cold that I fell down the cellar steps when I went down to get a bottle of shnapps to help us recover.

The Feast of St. John—a summer celebration. A puzzling array of voices and faces in constant motion. Voices that continued all night through, long after the bonfire was burnt out. Yells and laughter that could still be heard, that kept on speaking, even though it was years ago. Faces in all different stages of life and happiness, shapes disappearing down through the yard like they did back then, standing with glasses in their hands on the lawn; and towards the small hours, sitting around the table in front of the burnt-out fire. And who, hours later, still had not gone to bed, but now were out on the veranda in the clear morning sunshine. A St. John's celebration that still exists there at the house. Faces and voices and bodies still celebrating the Feast of St. John.

There must still be brambles with wild blackberries over by the hedgerow near the woods. They will still give berries this year, but it seems rather unreal. Reality back then was when, every so often, I made a detour over to them to see how far they had progressed. And finally one morning I walked over with a cardboard box that I filled with my pickings. With sour blackberries in my mouth I turned and looked between the trees out to the bog, where a duck hunter was rowing around in a boat. I could hear him shouting to his dog farther away across the calm water, and I could hear the dog whining with zeal as it splashed through the reeds.

The place in the woods where we killed the viper is still there. As is the stone down by the beach that we sat on. But is all completely different now.

Together with the married couple, who are now considering renting the house, I looked at the rooms upstairs. She walked around with her handbag hugged tight to her body with both hands, scrutinizing the dust and any dilapidation. We looked in the last room; it was empty like the others.

"Wild grapes grow over the window in the summer," I said. "The whole house will look green from the outside, and sometimes you have to prune them to open the windows. They are full of birds nests. Once there was a gray sparrow that came in on that table there."

"They're nice rooms," she said.

On the dressing table stood a bronze figurine—a beetle, as big as a hand, with wings that opened. I had seen it every day for a few months without it really registering, and forgot about it. It was still there, and now I remembered it.

"Aunt Olga could stay in this room," she said.
Her husband nodded.

That room had been mine.

September 1939

It was the beginning of September, and the beach season was over, but the water was still so warm that we swam several times a day. And when we swam, out in the water directly opposite us to the west we could see the twin bluffs of Skarreklit protruding above the waves, pretending it was Bornholm, here in the North Sea on Denmark's sandy west coast. In the evening the sun went down behind Bulbjerg and Skarreklit, making them stand out in silhouette.

It is always a bit strange being a beach-goer this time of year, but that September it felt especially strange. The beach was completely deserted, and the North Sea's waves came rolling in at the bay of Jammerbugten, smashing their crests into the shore and yielding to the side. It was as if it were something new for the North Sea to be looked at in this way—with a beach-goer's eyes. There was a clarity of autumn and September over the beach. It was lonesome, swimming around in the water, and even more lonesome looking out toward the peaks of Skarreklit and Bulbjerg. Going home from the beach gave the feeling of being the absolutely last beach-goer, following every other beach-goer that had already gone home long ago. In West Jylland, you don't recognize the approaching winter by the trees' losing their leaves; you recognize it by the beaches losing their bathers. They disappear, leaving behind a wooden shutter over the opening to the ice cream stand, and otherwise: stillness.

No beach-goers ever come to the place I'm talking about anyway. It lies midway between Svinkløv and Bulbjerg, and the beach is just a high barrier of pebbles bordering the heather and some tufts of lyme grass. The bottom slants abruptly down into the water, so it's impossible to touch bottom just a few yards out, and the waves roll in, one after another, smacking their foreheads into the barrier. It resounds, "Whung!" and then all the stones give way, rattling. And "Whung!" and they rattle again. That's why there are never any bathers. When I have been there before, during the busy season, the difference in beach life has hardly been noticeable. Nevertheless it has been different. At that time I always had an awareness of vacation and high summer and thronging beach life. And when I was up at the post office, where there is also a telephone switchboard, a barber shop and a store, buying licorice felt different too. It was a licorice tape that I stuffed into myself like one does on summer vacations, even though it tastes terrible. But that month in 1939 it was completely different. When I chewed on a licorice tape in the clear September air, it was as if it had been left behind by a sun-burned girl in shorts, that now long ago had returned to the city. And the licorice tape didn't only taste bad, but also very sad, as if it were the last licorice tape in the world.

Spread apart over the heather there are only three houses. Sørensen's and Kristensen's are low, rust-red and straw-thatched. They are both farmers and fishermen. Laursen's is white and slate-roofed; he's a carpenter and a fisherman. And up by the county road, a half-mile away, is Niels Post's house. He's not a fisherman; he runs the post office, telephone switchboard, barbershop and store.

We fished during the day, and sometimes at night too, and the boats lay pulled up on land between the barrier of stones and the poor tufts of hay and heather. We hoisted our boat up with a hand crane, and laid wooden rollers under it. It took twenty minutes to get it out in the water, while two gray sheep with black faces circled around in their tethers just behind us and knew neither toil nor trouble. When we had walked our feet sore on the pebbles and the boat was finally in the water, it was always astonishing to see it at last in its right element. The motor was started, and steadily and rhythmically it thumped us out through the surf, fanned the waves to the side and jumped over them, while we sat and rested, watching the beach sway behind us. Sørensen's, Kristensen's and Laursen's homes became just insignificant houses on a long coastline.

Søren sat with his foot on the tiller, so he had his hands free to tend to the motor now and then. Once fishermen looked out across the waves and up to their sail; now they look with the same gaze out across the waves and down at their motor. Sometimes we watched the lobster traps being tended, and if there were lobsters in them, they were taken to be sold. But if there were crabs, they tossed them to us, because there was no one else who would bother to eat them.

We were the same age: the two fishermen, Søren and Laust; and the two beach-goers: my friend and I. We were all about thirty or so. We had been getting together for years and years, and we enjoyed each other's company. We used to beat up on one another in huge wrestling matches on the Kristensen's washroom floor, dividing ourselves into teams, competing for several hours at a time. Søren and Laust have never gotten over the gags that we other two are always playing. If we do something crazy, everyone laughs so hard the boat is about to split in half. When one day, with able-bodied mien, I walked across the deck, slipped on a flounder and landed on a cod, Søren laughed himself blue in the face and the boat went ninety degrees off course. He doesn't mean any harm, though. When he writes to me, he always writes that he wishes all the best to me and mine: *Respectfully, Søren Sørensen*.

When we weren't fishing or swimming, there was a pine woods in which we could go for a walk, and by the spots of feathers on the forest floor we could see where the fox had been at work since last time. There was also the walk along the beach to Bulbjerg, the walk along the beach to Svinkløv, or the walk down the sandy, pot-holed farm road, with heather between the tracks and spots of red, iron-filled soil, up to the county road where we could have a card game with Niels Post. In the fishermen's houses by the beach it's sinful to play drinking games, but at Niels Post's place by the county road it's not only not sinful, it's fun. The oil lamp was set on the plush tablecloth, and Niels Post's wife tended the telephone switchboard, the post office, the barbershop, and the store in the meantime; and she could still knit socks at the same time. Fifteen years ago she served us fruit compote on the plush tablecloth when we came in the evening. Now it was Niels who served us, and it wasn't fruit compote anymore. In the evening on the walk home the moon shone over the fields, and the night air was so fresh and still, that as we crossed from Niels Post's door over the cement road, and on the path home, there were no other sounds to be heard than the very soft, gentle sound of our shoes in the powder of the wheel tracks, or perhaps a horse or a cow stomping on the grass off to the side, or a sheep that picked up its head in the dark, watching as we passed.

When we fished at night we slept during the day; but when we had slept at night, then we would get up at five in the morning. The morning freshness rushed to meet us when we came outside. It's as if we wake up in many different stages: first we wake to light, indoors. When we go outside, we discover another wakefulness. We wake to all the smells. We wake up to life and it seems new and wonderful. As we open the door we discover that we've only got one half; the other half is delivered to us when we cross the threshold.

We ambled over the farmyard, and from the kitchen window we heard water being pumped. From the cage over the workshop we heard the cheerful sounds of pigeons. The heather was wet with dew, and on the trail from the east we saw Søren and Laust walking towards us— Søren in front with his red hair and a sheepish morning smile on his face. The two sheep down by the boat had damp coats. Skarreklit still lay there to the west. The pebbles jingled sharply in our ears, and the North Sea was a sea of morning dew washing against the coast.

So there we sat again in the boat—the last day we sat like that. Suddenly we saw five blackish-grey cruisers come up from the west over Jammerbugten with black smoke billowing low behind them all the way out to the horizon.

It was the first time we saw them, but it seemed like these threatening ships had moved through our minds many times before. That September it was common knowledge that war had broken out. It made the stillness in the September days even more still. It made the peacefulness under the high clear sky into a church aisle. It created devotion, with the sight of the sheep that lay in the lyme grass looking at you with black, god-adoring faces, and with the sight of the pigeons that flew away with a flash of silver under their wings. It was as if it made each thing an ending to all things, and that September an ending to all previous summers. A fissure opened in our consciousness, and it was as if the two parts had shifted in relation to one another. It was precisely these days, when our thoughts were moving forgetfully in both parts; it was desconcerting.

I sat in the boat laughing, and suddenly, sorrow's smoke billows appeared, spreading their silence as fast as an injection in my blood. Then I looked down onto my laughter as onto an orchestra pit, looked at the faces surrounding me that I'd never really appreciated before....

While we stared at the cruisers traveling northwards, we heard the sound of the motor of our own boat—the explosions and piston strokes so distracting and distinct as if it were these sounds, and not the silent ships on the horizon, that were new to us.

"Englishmen!" said Søren, as he sat with his one knee bent over the tiller. The waves went under us, lifted us up, and the metallic smacks rang as did the pulse beats from the exhaust pipe in the cool sunshine.

"Out there was where they fought in the last war. We could hear it up and down the whole coast."

"I was confirmed in a tuxedo," said Laust. He laughed uncomfortably. "And it was the same day he drifted in, that sailor...."

We looked again at the cruisers, and the ocean wasn't the same, not until only the smoke billows were visible on the horizon.

That evening we paid Laursen, the carpenter-fisherman, because we were going to leave the next morning. He told us about the sailor who had drifted ashore back then—a sailor in a foreign uniform and a sailor's collar and nothing much else. One Sunday morning he lay at the ocean's edge, where the waves come and smack their foreheads into the barrier of stones, making them rattle. He lay just next to where the boat is pulled ashore, and there probably had also been sheep on their tethers a couple of yards away back then. When Laursen spoke about it, he always pointed out the fact that the foreigner was a fisherman, as if that were the point of the story. He was a private, and an older man, and Laursen maintained that it was because he was a fisherman.

Maybe he also came from a place where the boats were pulled up by hand and where sheep walked in the heather behind them.

A Hunting Trip

When the young Greenlandic boys asked me for cigarettes, usually by forming a circle and looking at my hands expectantly, as a dog would, I handed them out. But there were limits to my unethicalness. I always asked how old they were, and, not without pride of my knowing how to count in Greenlandic, I noted the age of each one before giving him the cigarette. If one was under nine, I said *namik!* to him, which meant that he couldn't have any, and I passed by his Eskimo nose.

If he still held out his hand, silently pleading with irresistible brown eyes, I sternly lifted my index finger, the very symbol of ethics, and repeated: *Namik! Kommunaraad kramapok!* which elicited wild fraternal cheering from all the 11-, 12- and 13-year olds. That's right. The Council got angry when children smoked cigarettes.

Eventually I got used to having a train of little men following me when I wandered around in the area surrounding the colony. We tramped off, clouds of smoke trailing behind us, in no rush, ready for anything. They always came uninvited—walking on my heels, turning when I turned, stopping when I stood still—but still displaying, until I had approved of their company, a very reserved and unintrusive presence by not being able to see over my waist. Apparently, they were out taking a walk with my legs. As long as they avoided looking me in the eye, they couldn't be any bother, could they?

They were the epitome of cordiality if I showed the slightest provocation. Then their dark eyes and white teeth gleamed in smiles that nothing could erase. When they said something, and I understood what it was, they laughed, and their faces beamed with excitement and glee. When I didn't understand and shook my head, even though they repeated and repeated what it was, they laughed too, bending in half from the immense comic effect, and in the end having to hold their stomachs and sit down, incapacitated from laughing.

When I asked two boys to row me out onto the fjord, the dinghy was unseaworthy, and full as a commuter bus, before we set off. Laughing was no extravagance for them—it was the most natural form of life expression. They stood there rowing with big ingenuous smiles, white teeth and happy, dark eyes. When there was something to laugh at, they laughed. Smiles were simply the readiness to laugh. And when there was nothing to laugh at, oftentimes they laughed anyway. As if through a safety valve, a surplus of the joy of life bubbled out of their mouths.

I sat with my rifle, towering adult-like over the crowd, feeling like the Nile God in the midst of all that fertility.

I can still see them, jumping around on the hummocks with their bowed legs in worn-out workpants. But I have also seen them, at times, become distant and mature in their expression, without their being aware of it themselves, when with the hunting instinct of a hundred generations they took in the view of the fjord, looking for wild prey.

But when there was nothing to shoot there was plenty of frivolity, which was easy to laugh at. And when we at last caught sight of some birds out over the still, blue water, that wasn't so bad either. Then they bubbled over with delight, literally squealing with expectation and enthusiasm for the hunt.

Seagulls many! they exclaimed with suppressed rapture, and they became quieter the closer we approached. Finally the whole noisy excursion bus was silent and charged with excitement and suppressed breathing. Only their distant expressions showed under the anorak hoods, or under the thick skullcaps of shiny blue-black hair, conveying the enjoyment of the hunt. Eyes sought other eyes in absolute silence redoubling the delight of fellowship and solidarity.

This could deteriorate into wide-scale murder. Here it must be mentioned that in Greenland, the same rules that exist at home about not shooting sitting animals, and not shooting more than one at a time, do not apply. Those are rules to conserve wildlife. In Greenland you conserve your cartridges. Wildlife is food. Even seagulls are food for both people and dogs, and obtaining food in the least expensive way is a matter of life and death. Eventually, we approached a small glacial iceberg where 30 or 40 seagulls were sitting in a straight line, side by side along a sharply cut edge, like on the ridge of a house.

Then the little Greenlandic boys became deadly serious, and the boat glided forward with noiseless oarstrokes. When the whole row looked diagonally down at me, I fired, and seven or eight of them tumbled down into the clear, green water at the foot of the white, floating iceberg. I shot at one of the survivors that had taken wing. It stopped mid-flight and tumbled head over tail down into the boat where it was received eagerly, like a mis-hit soccer ball landing in the crowd. A six-year-old squirt, down among the legs of the others, became its lucky overlord. He was so small that he had to use two hands to hold it, at which both he and all the others couldn't help but laugh. He grabbed it by the head and whipped its body in the air and it was dead. It took just a fraction of a second. Then he jumped up on the thwart with the corpse. Holding the dead bird up over his head, he made the white wings flap invitingly—see what good shape it's in? Now there wasn't anything to laugh at. His shrill seagull call leaped across the fjord, overtaking the fleeing birds, arriving promisingly and convincingly among them. He was so little that he couldn't even wipe his own nose. Sometimes his tongue snuck out, like an independently thinking being and took care of it, while he was unconscious of it—the wiping. But a hunter? *That* he was!

The swarm of seagulls, after fleeing out over the sun-drenched mountains of ice, stopped and returned. There were young, grey seagulls and white three-toed gulls called "tatteratter" that kept flying over the boat. Every time one of them was torn from the flock by a shot and splashed down into the water, like a piece of fruit shaken off of an invisible tree, the boys cheered and shouted, shrieking like seagulls, swinging ever more dead birds.

It must have sounded strange. A center of sound in the middle of the quiet fjord. The kind of place where a cloud of seagulls shrieking at the top of their lungs would congregate over a school of fish or some drifting trash. And yet there were none other than the seagulls and ourselves who heard any of it. The generators of noise were just a tiny spot in the great silence. The soundwaves reached no further than the first props in the great scenery. Iceberg after iceberg and glimmer after glimmer out over the fjord heard nothing at all. They have had the same millennium-old quietude, while the Greenlanders jumped around in the dinghy screaming themselves blue in the face, eliciting soundwaves in a little circle around themselves, but beyond that: silence. The Greenlandic enormity and span not only absorbs any volume of voice, it also absorbs oneself when one thinks about it. That thought, that the scenery continues on, not only where no voice can reach, but also thousands of miles where no one will ever even be seen. So oneself is swallowed up just as one's shout.

A sense of this reaches me when I think in distances and remote mountains and even remoter mountains behind them. It can also occur if I am in a boat, drifting in towards the side of an iceberg, touching it with my hand, leaning myself out over the railing and with my nose to the water glimpsing the nearest few meters of ice disappearing down under the flickering surface, then fading into a colorful play of milky blue, watery blue, and finally, the deepest blue.

And the gulls, sweeping past, over the boat, coming sailing in over the gun barrel, like swimming clumps of ice in the air—Why are they doing this? What Danish bird would act like that? But even this half-tame, unsuspecting flight towards death which the Greenland gulls perform, tell of the greatness of nature. Knock them down, hit them one after another, and we shoot down something in ourselves at the same time. We shrink before their trust and abundance, as we do before the icebergs' grandeur. They tell the truth without intentional insult. They make people feel small by never having seen one before.

A white malemuk tumbled down after a shot and sat on the water. Its one wing didn't sit so nicely on its body anymore, but it didn't seem to notice that anything was wrong. It wasn't scared. It sat high on the water, only a couple of meters away from us, and in its black eyes were only surprise and curiosity. It didn't attempt to swim away, just laid its head aslant to truly take in the view of the strange beings in the boat. It wasn't until a hand reached out for it that it got scared.

That was when I suddenly understood how Stone Age people, with bows and arrows, were able to shoot wild animals. It wasn't accuracy and stealth alone. When the animals outnumbered the people, the animals quietly let the people get close enough to shoot. The stag might once have stood still, observing the man approaching him. Even when it felt the arrow's effect between its ribs, it might not have understood that *it* was the target.

Greenlanders themselves avoid the scruples and sensitivities of a heavily laden conflict that the outsider might feel. They have a solidarity with the animals, as well as with the rest of nature. They also belong within nature. Especially in the Greenlanders' relationship to seals I have been able to observe emotions that approach sworn fellowship, and last beyond death. Fondness, and a millennial friendship, that a shot to the head of the animal does not injure. Death, where is your sting? I was inside an earthen hut to photograph a man and wife among their possessions. On the floor lay a freshly-killed seal. They sat themselves soberly on the platform bed to be photographed, but the seal, which they were proud of, they went over to, lifted it up by its fins and held its nice human-like head with forehead and whiskers up between them, so it could be in the picture too. They were all friends....

When I rowed home in the dinghy, one of the Greenlandic boys sat, patting a dead seagull that he had on his lap. Once, he looked up at me, his teeth revealing a white smile, and he searched for the Danish words...*tastes good!* he said. And his hand continued petting and caressing the white breast of the bird.

Inuit Nuna
The Land of the People

It's strange to think about afterwards. Do I feel like I visited a country and lived there?

I know that once I was lying in a chaise lounge on the deck of a ship and that I saw the white snow cap on the mountain by Umanak, gleaming golden in the sun. I know I made my way through landscapes in every direction, and rested in them too, lying anchored to their ground with my neck buried in heather. Multiple times.

But still I wasn't really *in* a country. I was a stranger. I didn't really live there. I collided with it. And the conflict is what remains. That is what remains after every trip. I can only report on how much like a stranger I felt, which I do now by telling to what I was a stranger.

My first impression of having Greenland under my feet, after 14 days of travel, was as if I were banging my head against a wall. A blow to the head, and then the great stillness! And I never got over that blow. The aftereffects still reside within me like a mildly foggy state of confusion. The few ideas I had attached to my consciousness beforehand shook loose like screws and have continued to rattle around, reminding me of their failure.

I had read everything I could find about Greenland, stuffed myself with preparatory knowledge, not only at home but also on the ship. After fourteen days of company in close quarters, with meals following tightly on one another's heels, the rustling of cards over the bridge tables, endless discussions, and a twinge of idleness, land finally appeared, to end the treadmill at last. Now the adventures would begin!

There it was—the great island—in real life. If my eyes weren't deceiving me, I was seeing several islets, shards of cliffs, small pieces of reality that honest green waves washed up and around. Greenland—Inuit Nuna—The Land of the People. And farther in the distance, steep cliffs with their feet in the white foam of the breakers.

Now the adventures would begin! With the speed of the voyage in my body I was prepared for even greater speed. With a companion

I walked immediately onto land and up into the mountains. We climbed and hiked, and fjords, lakes and sweeps of valleys fell and spread themselves below us like a magic map. Further upwards. As if by witchcraft, every step revealed new landscapes and perspectives. It was watery and desolate, a rain-threatened afternoon, and not a person in sight. Not a creature on the earth, not a bird under the firmament—only mountains sinking below us and airy emptiness over us, while we marched to the heavens. We hiked straight to the sky, swam in it. The earth sailed away into space beneath us. Then it started to rain, and we quickly moved to shelter between two massive cliffs. And that is where I felt the blow.

The stillness. The quiet. We still had the speed of the ship and the events of the trip inhabiting our restless bodies, and the delimitation and timelessness of this spot felt like a shock. Just this spot! This clump of heathland and this little mound with crowberries. It spread magically in our consciousness, grew to colossal import, drowned us in wonder. Thirty square feet of the giant globe, as incidental as possible, and yet so eternal as if it were the entire globe in itself. The whole time we had been traveling, this mound with its crowberries had been right here, and sometimes they bowed a bit in the wind, and some juices seeped up through them and nothing else happened. But that was plenty. Five years ago some things happened, and ten years ago some other things—emotions and coincidental events. Search through your life, think of anything. Regardless, this mound was here, moving in the wind just like right now.

All books back on the shelves. All book cabinets closed. From here emerged the great truth, our daily existence given to us from The Mystery.

While the rain closed off our view, we clung to this spot. Speed, events, and a thousand changing impressions—from the trip and before it—approached us like breakers, recoiled around us like a tide against a pier. And when we had sat there long enough, two small birds appeared, fluttering around, precisely over this spot as if they were home.

During this clashing of sensations of time, I felt like I could sense a fourth dimension. In this spiritual draft all book learning and handed-down knowledge was blown from me. I sat on the naked floor of my own awareness. Perhaps this was the only place on Greenland where I really *was*. Ever since, I have always had to see Greenland from that spot—with nature's immutability, millennial peace and everyday-ness as a backdrop. And in addition, the thought affected me so strongly and strangely that, regardless of what was happening around me in the world, that spot will always remain. I could find it again if I looked for it, and if I sat there for a while, a little bird would come fluttering to its familiar spot over the heather and crowberries.

I also think of the people of Greenland as if they were in a strange collision of varying time and cultural perceptions.

Greenlanders, in just a couple of centuries, have had to travel the millennia-long path from the Stone Age to modern technological society. The wild heathens who suddenly were presented with Christianity's and Civilization's gift of mercy. There is a painting of Hans Egede, where you see him kneeling in thankful prayer, just after he set foot on Greenland's coast. Or was it the highly-evolved communal society, the warm-hearted, humane cooperatives in the polar zone, which suddenly were flooded with Europe's ocean adventurers and terminologies? Isn't it typical that Hans Egede had numerous convicts with him, both male and female, to help colonize and enlighten the Eskimos? With all due respect to Hans Egede's courage and selflessness, it is laughable to think about that fact. This was the opportunity for the Eskimo to learn about immorality. Hans Egede imprinted it on them indelibly, and the released convicts also taught them a thing or two. The royal Danish priest preached the idealistic message of Christianity, and simultaneously was pulled back by the hem of his priestly garments by the royal Danish government. It's not worth it! They threatened to shut down the mission if it didn't start producing economic benefits.

Since then, Denmark has had the honor of never demanding economic benefit from its colony.

But it must have caused a good deal of confusion among the Greenlanders. I can just see it. There are certain things that were over their heads back then. And I still think I can glimpse some of that confusion today, in controlled and polite form, like a silence in certain moments, as if the innermost kernel in their kind beings still is a question, a question whose unanswerableness they have gotten used to through the generations.

It is possible to walk up high mountains and get a good sense of the Greenland landscapes. But it is not possible to walk up a mountain and get a good sense of the population. What can usually be used to assess a people—their development and production—holds no sway here, due to the Greenlanders' lack of responsibility for their development and production. Despite the Greenlandic magazines, despite the Council and spiritual life, the Greenlandic people, seen through the eyes of others, move in a peculiar manner, as if beneath their own surface. People of mixed race, along the edge of the icecap, are difficult to get a handle on. The interaction of so many factors such as race-mixing, altered living conditions, cultural revolution, etc. has made the resulting individual into a roll of the dice. The results lay across the spectrum, the variations more evident than in other places. I have seen people with a highly developed cultural sense and rich intelligence mixed with a character of honorable primitivity, as if everything beneficial was inherited from both sides and none of the detrimental. And I have seen spiritual darkness and primitively impoverished ways of life paired with brazen street urchin morals, distrust, and mendaciousness, as if only the worst traits of both races and cultures were passed on.

I remember Greenlanders in crowds and in boats for an enthusiastic welcome when the Agency's whaling ship arrived hauling a whale, or when the ship *Disko*, another of the year's big events, arrived at the colony. Laughing, upturned faces, a warmth all the way down to my toes from sheer fellowship. Also, I remember another sight at such an event, a Greenlander in a kayak, wearing a fur, wet and gleaming with spray and seawater from the Davis Strait, rowing himself home with a newly shot seal—a sight from ancient times streaming out from between all the colorful dinghies. And he didn't turn his head towards the newly arrived ship. And just that—that he didn't think it worth his while to give as much as one glance to the Agency's ship—that has anchored itself in my memory with all of its potential interpretations. Making land, he stepped out of his kayak, lifted it up on his arm and carried it away. Then he retrieved the seal, but still without one look, still with his back to us. A ghost? He defied reality in two alternatives. Either he wasn't there, or we weren't there.

I remember one Greenlander who did a day hike with me as a friendly gesture, with no thought of reward, free and equal. And I didn't feel obligated to give him any money afterwards, but offered him a gift, and what happened? I was given a gift in return, and the trip with the Greenlander has remained ever since in the realm of unforgettableness. That is how marvelous it can be to receive a gift! Belief in one's fellow human being! A handshake across the oceans! A new and better Union of Peoples! And then I remember another who was going to be our guide for such and such a sum. Up and at 'em! What energy! Ready to conquer the distant mountains! But the terrain was not suited to this blitzkrieg. Half an hour later he was hobbling and had to rest, eagerly suggesting that we break for lunch, take a short nap and return home. Well, those mountains were quite far away! Incredibly so! And it seemed that he had sprained his foot. Big drama. Might I trade rifles with him? Why not. Then what would I say to giving him my slacks?

I saw young Greenlanders who had been in Denmark, and some of them remained simply Greenlandic hunters, but with an augmentation of Danish West Coast fisherman, both in bearing and in technical proficiency, so they ended up right in the middle of what modern Greenland needs in a seal hunter. But a couple of them had changed into incurable comedians. All the tools of civilization were at their disposal but inwardly they were just jokesters, with the exact personality needed to maneuver decorously and continually with cane, hat and gloves.

And even with all this, I am not saying that even the worst-behaved of the Greenlanders is not better than many of the "civilized" they came in contact with. It is said that when Cook returned to human society after his North Pole Expedition, to each of the two Eskimos who had left their wives and children to serve him for over a year, he gave a box of matches. And there was no use in their complaining.

The variations in the results of cultural development in Greenland are stark.

But it is possible to get a sense of the causation behind the development. There is a clinking of tin from food cans, and barrels rolling heavily over warehouse floors in modern Greenland. But, still emanating from the young boys' cheerful faces and resounding shouts, is the spirit of the chase, necessary to propel the harpoon towards the walrus, when it thunders out of the water to attack the parchment-thin kayak. And behind the ancient people's tensed faces there is a sense of the rediscovered wisdom gleaned from generations of independent survival in the polar land. It is as if the very young and the very old somehow have a connection to creation. They are either not bought into the development yet, or they have turned away from its graph. They retain something of the infants' and the elderly's prehistoric timelessness. They are like the day-old heather flowers in the mountains or the centuries-old mountains themselves. And, as if through a reversed binoculars, they appear before us revealing a Greenland that exists outside of time.

The Window Ajar

Normally we hunker down in our daily lives. Every day has enough of its annoyances—everyday annoyances. When we involve ourselves with problems that reach beyond the daily and adjacent horizon, we do it half-reluctantly, as if we have to get over something unpleasant, and as quickly as possible return to our inner circles again. We keep our noses in our private chess games.

But at certain moments in our lives this changes. Then, it is as if we get permission and are demanded by the situation to lift our gaze. This happens for example, for most of us, when we stand by an open grave. Three shovels full of earth are suddenly the only sounds in the world, just accentuating the silence we know always has been, and the silence we know will come one day. We feel it as if a lid has been taken off of our existence. Our private daily life is suddenly made distant and unimportant. We are pulled from the routine up to a higher level, the level of poets and thinkers, where we thoughtfully survey humanity. Then we hunker down again. Good thing it didn't last too long.

At an open grave, or at New Year's Eve under the stars when the year turns, we get a faint sense and we shiver. Whew. Let's put on our hats and leave the cemetery, let's go back into the living room and the warmth, out of the New Year's Eve night, and wash it down with a drink, put on a mask and blow in a toy trumpet.

I remember how New Year's was received in my childhood home. I remember all the way back to when my grandfather led the ceremony—and I was very little back then, since he died in 1913. It made an impression. I remember the stout old man with a white beard and a black corduroy skullcap on his head at that moment when the grandfather clock, which is now standing in my living room, began the twelve tolls. He did peculiar things. With a lit candle in his hand he opened a window out to the pitch black winter night.

"Thus we let out the old year and let in the new year," he said. And when he had closed the window again, he added like an epilogue, "It is in God's hands what the year will bring."

And the cold night penetrated the room like a shiver—like it really was the new year making its entrance.

I do not think it was because this ceremony lay outside of the everyday routine that it imprinted itself on the consciousness of a boy only four years old. I believe it was because of the unusual mood of the adults—the difference in them—that in a flash it registered in the mind of a child, and the occurrences were imprinted. It was the hush, the solemnity, the humility of the adults in those few seconds that made the impression. They were not like adults usually were; they were no longer in charge. They stood like they were being subjected to something, like someone else was in charge of them.

This was, as I mentioned, before 1914.

What was the fate they in those seconds felt so heavily burdened by? How long could their sense and imagination have fumbled in absolutely correct acknowledgment of being small and uncertain, subject to greater powers and to events over which they had no control? What was it they let out; what was it they let in? It could have been worries and hopes concerning sickness and health, economy, the children's future, etc. More vague and distant it could have been adversity in general—you never know what might happen—something could befall us at any time like lightning from a clear blue sky. That war could be imminent? Hardly. That risk, that possibility has always been too distant, too absurd for a healthy thoughtful person to occupy himself with. But my grandfather's thoughts probably did extend to the King and the whole royal family. If he had materialized his vague feeling it would have stretched to people at sea in general, on all the world's oceans—a prayer for them, because he was an old sailor himself.

Proximate things, all of them, it seems now. And on top of that, still more vague, the feeling of general incomprehensibility must have loomed—the acknowledgement of immense vastness and our own pitifulness and inadequacy. But these were proximate things they had to take from reality as they knew it—and back then, they still could know it.

Reality, back then, was almost something comforting in itself, I think. Something real and understandable, observable like the mechanism in a bicycle frame. Something you could talk about. Though it might be maltreated, it could always be repaired again.

And what has the stack of calendars with advancing years brought us since then? What will have snuck darkly into our minds when we this year lift our noses from the proximate? Because in these seconds a year is being replaced by another, and we make a weak head-shaking attempt to understand our existence and our circumstances here on earth.

What has been let out and in since then?

Two World Wars of such magnitude that hardly anyone before then had possessed sufficient fearful tendencies to be able to imagine them. Both conducted under many intense, grim hopes. The first in order to, among other things, bring an end to all wars. The second to give people freedom from fear. And in the bargain, we have a world where fear—or the reasons for fear—are still on the rise, nearing apocalyptic proportions. Since the reasons for fear are so strong, so well-founded, most people refuse to look them in the eyes. Instead they quickly turn away from the fearful premonitions, hurry to put on a paper mask and comic glasses, and continue with their immediate and cozy lives as if nothing were happening.

And the paper masks are called self-assurance, arrogance, conventional thought, superciliousness, nonchalance and indifference. They are found in all these shades and in combination, and the glasses are called lack of imagination and torpor. In this get-up one can shout starry-eyed and naive at those less-disguised.

We refuse to look apocalyptic danger in the eyes; we suppress it from our thoughts. Or, if we send it a glance and give it a thought, we hope—although we previously have experienced that fearful misgivings have been fulfilled and fulfilled to excess—that this time it is too terrible to actually occur.

And besides, "To whom God has given a task, God has also given ability." We have certainly only smiled before at this old-fashioned belief that smells like a musty emanation from a civil servant, but we put our trust or at least our hope in it anyway, if only this once.

Of course there are people who deal with this, people in high office as they are called, who work with things like this, trying to avert them.

And we forget, or don't realize, that God has not given that amount of ability to anyone. The man on the street, the scientist, the politician—none of these has enough perspective on these things or enough imagination to grasp the extent of their impact.

No human imagination or brilliance is enough these days.

The world is not the same as it was.

Reality was once as simple and manageable as a bicycle frame. Today "reality" is only an antiquated word. Who can conceive it—who can look at it? It is beyond our reach. It circles around us, we hear its signals, but not one of us comprehends them. Reality has become unreal. It is as if the scientists have abolished it in order to bring back blind fate. But politicians—the responsible ones—the world over negotiate and bargain with reality as if it still were something they could understand. And meanwhile it grows over our heads like an irresponsible chain reaction.

The world and reality have changed. When the first atomic bomb was produced, Einstein remarked that now we need a change of consciousness, if mankind is going to survive. He had the imagination to break with previous schools of thought, broke through the shell of reality at the time. He had a first glimpse of what lay beyond, and brought that message back—that now everything was different, that now among the general population a break from previous trains of thought was necessary—a change of consciousness—if humanity was going to survive.

We would hardly call him starry-eyed and naive, would we?

But what has become of this general change of consciousness? We could search for it for a long time.

We search for it while those in power undertake actions that at first glance don't appear to make sense, given the situation. What are these strange things they are letting in for us? Letting them in without ceremony, without lit candles, or the chance to reflect. Just the window discretely ajar for a moment and then closed again. And there we stand and something new has entered the room, something fateful or malodorous or both, something that makes everything more uncomfortable. But within a few days we get used to it. It gets forgotten, blends into the routine.

And furthermore, their actions are done with the best of intentions. We are sure of this. Really. It is done as a continuation of the still ongoing, far-reaching attempt to secure for humanity freedom from fear.

The problem is just the method…it's been tried before. It's old hat. And so far it has worked counter to its aim.

Due to the fears we harbor in ourselves, we create fear for others, which creates more fear for ourselves, and so on and so on.

And the bombs grow in number and size and keep growing and growing. And more or less authorized masqueraders hold preparedness speeches for us. Everything isn't as bad as you think .If an atomic bomb is dropped, just tip over a table and lay down, so the table top comes between you and the bomb.

A vicious circle. We continue to use circular logic in a world that has become four-dimensional. Only in one sense does it give the result that can lead to freedom from fear: if there is no one left to feel it.

But if by freedom from fear we mean the possibility to *live* in security, then it gets difficult fast. A change in consciousness is needed. I think Einstein was right. And it is not only necessary that others change—that our opponents change—we also have to change ourselves.

But what does this mean, and how should it happen? We stand fumbling. But I have a sense that it is necessary to make way for this new attitude, that we gather the courage to look fear in the eyes and not hide ourselves under the comforter of our daily routine, not resign ourselves to let others deal with it—because then we may be taking from them the possibility of resolving it. We must stretch imaginations and perceptions as far and as universally as possible—even though it is nowhere near enough. We must get ourselves together and try to grasp our fate—and not just at ceremonious opportunities like the turning of the year—but for everyday use.

Ultimately we must realize however unfamiliar, however new, however risky it may feel, that while enmity breeds only enmity and mistrust breeds only mistrust, trust—the most elementary, innate human form of reconciliation—is the only thing that can create trust. And that it can be done.

The Wind in West Jylland

The sound of the wind belongs to West Jylland. And that sound is part of my childhood. The wind gives West Jylland landscapes voice and life: it whistles in the lyme grass, whispers in the heather, buzzes in windows and doors, and sings in the telegraph wires. You can lie beside a West Jylland road, just listening to the unceasing wind, listening to it for hours, because it is speaking on your behalf in its human-like tone: whining, sighing, resigned, sometimes desperate, then subsiding to easy chatter. Even when expounding as freely as possible, it is still as if it were somehow restricted, and fighting a difficult battle with itself.

The wind gives the ocean voice too. If you listen for it, you can hear the sea from over a mile away. Its thunder sets the mood of expectation.

I worked my way out towards the ocean through wide rows of sand dunes. The dunes are already oceans themselves, an ocean in tumult, waves that have solidified after having gone ashore. The lyme grass whispers, swaying in the wind, while bluebells and yellow hawkweed hunker down in the depressions. Plumes of sand come gusting over the crests, blowing sand in my mouth and in my eyes. Every time I reach a new peak I think that now I must be there, but a new dune sea, new waves of sand appear.

And then I stand on the farthest dune and see it once more—the North Sea. It is ebb tide, and the water has retreated. Bent over, I stride across the deserted beach to near the breakers. The roar is borne freely here, without the dunes in between. I am filled with wind and sound. There is song in the air! The hard stretch of beach trembles like an organ as the waves come streaming, smacking their foreheads into the escarpment. Under my feet the ground lurches like from the impact of a battering ram.

The ringing of the waves, the foam of the breakers, and the hooting of the wind. This is what I call ocean! Shall I lift my voice and shout along? But the gale plugs my mouth, fills my lungs to bursting before I can get a word in—and it wouldn't have been audible anyway. It would have been drowned in this wide-ranging spectrum of atonal, harmonic, rising and falling sounds.

    The most formidable nature in Denmark. At one point the sun finds a peephole through the sinister banks of clouds, and far out to sea a section of the dark ocean suddenly becomes bottle-green and summer-like, warm and inviting to the eye, with chalk-white foam in the twinkling sunshine. Then sunlight and shadow begin to interchange, following on one another's heels across the shore, marching off across the row of dunes, holding a lighting rehearsal with stark changes between gray weekday and carefree Sunday. It works satisfactorily, but must be for later use. The projector is turned off, and ocean and shore return to a gray gloom. For a moment the glints of sun continue along a shoreline within myself, but then they are lost there too, and on both reality's and my soul's shore only storm-battered overcast weather remains.

    A border of greasy foam lies stranded on the beach, where the water no longer reaches. The wind tousles it, shakes some flakes loose and chases them high up into the dunes. And then there are the stones—worn round—gray, brown and blue, to which some of them seaweed has attached, stretching out and turning like weathervanes in the sand. I recognize that too.

    There is a painting by Jens Søndergård of a man standing by the North Sea. He is looking out over the water with his hands in his pockets, leaning forward at an angle completely at odds with the law of gravity, obviously a man who is about to fall, already well on his way down towards the sand. Yet he remains hanging there, held up by the gale. That is how you stand at the North Sea. Turn your head and your hair raises up, swept by the wind like the seaweed on the stones.

    You stand leaning against the gale, under the element's power, have to guide your breathing so you don't get suffocated by too large a mouthful. Sometimes you hear nothing but the whoosh around yourself. The wind is playing on your body like on an instrument—drumming on your clothing, whistling through your nostrils and earlobes, howling in the corners of your mouth—new instrumental peculiarities at every change in position. And when you have adjusted yourself to the angle that provides a hiatus to the sounds around your person, then you hear the ocean's sinister tone in all its purity, reaching you all at once from the surf. Your ear is suddenly out there in the water, washed over like a shell by every showering wave, swept back and forth in the breakers, polished against the sand and water in the ocean's heavy rhythm.

A seagull, a large bird, ponderous as a stork in its wingbeats, comes sailing by, beating to windward along the shore. Its head is lifted, scouting out past the breakers. It is in no hurry. It's not after sticklebacks. It's wingbeats are few. At one point it stops flapping completely, gliding from then on without visible movement, much less effort, a hundred yards further into the gale, straight ahead against the—to all appearances—unceasing wind.

The bird turns the broadsides of its wings, allowing itself to be tossed over backwards, until it again reaches the line of surf, and resumes working the coastline in its search. Its scouting across the ocean gives it the same empty stare and movements, the same distant, imperturbable professionalism, that can be observed in fishermen. There is only ocean, eyes and reflexes.

Then it disappears—the only living thing—and this doubles the sensation of loneliness.

I was up in the Bovbjerg lighthouse, tramped up the ringing iron spiral staircase. There I was slowly explained the ingenious system of huge prisms, and the warmth from the night just past radiated off of them, evoking sweat and difficulty breathing. Then I opened the exterior door to the catwalk and there the wind hit me, slammed the iron door shut and tumbled me against the wall, refreshing as a shower, an all-powerful loving embrace: the northwest wind! Spread out below me lay a long stretch of West Jutland—this depressing, magnificent land. The gray, dead-straight coastline stretched endlessly, edged with lace by the breakers.

Twelve churches were visible from up there with the naked eye, over twenty with the help of binoculars, adding the most northerly up in Thy to the most southerly down around Vemb. By climbing 75 feet up, suddenly 15 miles of the desolate, slightly hilly landscape is revealed: the desert-like surfaces which shadows wander across, and of which every square foot now lies silent, subjected to familiar force by its fate—the eternal wind.

When I had walked out towards the dunes down a road that could hardly be called a road, a little tanned boy came tumbling out to me from a house that could hardly be called a house. "And where are you going?" he asked. "I'm going out to the ocean," I answered. "Will you come and visit us when you're done?" he asked, and I explained that I wasn't going to do that, since, of course, I didn't know them. But when I returned later on the same road, the little boy was standing there by the dented wall of the house, fingers in his mouth, staring out at me. And inside, behind the small windows, there were other faces turned outwards to the wonderment: someone went by.

The West Coast and the North Sea evoke more prodigious sensations and recollections than any other Danish natural environment. They persist in my memories from earliest childhood. If I walked twenty steps from our house, I saw the gray surface of the water in Esbjerg wharf, and in Grådyb between Fanø and Blåvands Huk, where fishing boats were sailing out to sea and inward towards shore. I remember a day with floodwaters, my father dressed in oilskin, even though he wasn't a fisherman, but a wholesaler. The water was rising by the hour, foot by foot. Huge waves tumbled over the English Wharf, where the warehouse buildings were, filling the cellars, crashing against the building walls, sweeping boats far inland, overturning railroad cars from their tracks. Ladies of Esbjerg's bourgeoisie were on their knees alongside the fishermen's wives, praying for mercy on life and property, while the storm reigned unforgettably over the city with a ceaselessly rising and falling harp-like tone.

Acknowledgements

Grateful acknowledgment is made to the editors of the following periodicals, where these essays first appeared, some in slightly different versions:

Asymptote: "A Man and his Great-Grandfather"
Badlands: "The Glint of Blue"
BODY Journal: "The Black Swan"
The Chattahoochee Review: "Sleep"
em-review: "Encounter with the Dark"
The Literary Review: "Deer Park in the Dark" and
                       "A Ride with a Lady"
Lowestoft Chronicle: "Safari on Mors Island"
The Missing Slate: "The Window Ajar"
Meat for Tea: "A Journey in 1944"
Puerto del Sol: "Addiction to speed"
Reunion: The Dallas Review: "The Horse on the Beach"

Danish Essay Titles and Original Publication Dates

Fartens narkomani (Addiction to speed) ©1964; Den Sorte Svane (The Black Swan) ©1964;

Dyrehaven i mørke (Deer Park in the Dark) ©1946; Mødet med mørket (Encounter with the Dark) ©1964; De Blå Glimt (The Glint of Blue) ©1964; Hvidtjørnen (The Hawthorns) ©1950; Et ridt med en dame (A Ride with a Lady) ©1946 ; Safari på Mors   (Safari on Mors Island) ©1950; En rejse i 1944 (A Journey in 1944) ©1969; Stumper af et spejl (Fragments of a Mirror) ©1969; En mand og hans oldefar (A Man and His Great-Grandther) ©1946; Hesten i strandkanten (The Horse on the Beach)   ©1950; Søvnen (Sleep) ©1946; Hængebøgen (The Weeping Beech) ©1950; Fortrydelsens genfærd (The Specter of Regret) ©1957; Tredive år efter (Thirty Years Later)©1964;Forsvundne somre (Vanished Summers) ©1946; September 1939 ©1946; En jagttur (A Hunting Trip) ©1941; Inuit Nuna (Inuit Nuna - The Land of the People) ©1941; Vinduet på klem (The Window Ajar) ©1964; Blæsten i vestjylland (The Wind in West Jylland) ©1950.

En jagttur and *Inuit Nuna* originally published by Jespensen og Pios. All other titles originally published by Gyldendal.

Knud Sønderby (1909-1966) was an eminent Danish novelist, journalist, translator, and essayist. The initial printing of his first novel, *Midt i en Jazztid (In the Middle of a Jazz Age)* sold out in fourteen days due to its immediate popularity among the youth of Denmark. Today this novel is his best-known work and an integral piece of the Danish literary canon. For two decades Sønderby wrote as a journalist for three major newspapers while publishing four additional novels and six plays, as well as translating numerous works into Danish for the Royal Theater. The essays in this volume are drawn from his six essay collections. Sønderby was also a founding member of the Danish Academy.

Founder of Hammer and Horn Productions, **Michael Goldman** promotes and produces translated works of Danish literature. Over one hundred of Goldman's translations of poetry and prose have appeared in literary journals such as Rattle, Harvard Review, World Literature Today, and International Poetry Review. The Midwest Book Review calls his series of poetry audiobooks "superb choices for connoisseurs of multicultural poetry, worthy of the highest recommendation." His translated book publications include *Farming Dreams* by Knud Sørensen, *Average Neuroses* by Marianne Koluda Hansen, and *Stories about Tacit* by Cecil Bødker. He lives in Florence, Massachusetts, USA. hammerandhorn.net

www.ingramcontent.com/pod-product-compliance
Lightning Source LLC
Chambersburg PA
CBHW021440080526
44588CB00009B/620